iREACH™

How to Market Your
OUTREACH

DR. RAY HAMPTON

How to Market Your
OUTREACH

DR. RAY HAMPTON

For inquiries write to Attention: Dr. Ray Hampton email address
(dr.rayhampton@seattledreamcenter.org)

Seattle International Dream Center
www.seattledreamcenter.org

Edited & Formatted by:
Hunter Heart Publishing
www.hunterheartpublishing.com

Cover Design: Chevy Cortez
www.chevycortez.com

ISBN-13: 978-0-9797679-0-6
ISBN-10: 0-9797679-0-3

Printed in the United States of America

MEET DR. RAY HAMPTON

RAY HAMPTON was born in Oahu, Hawaii on October 8, 1964 and is the oldest of six siblings: Damon, Herbert, Ralph, Arlene and Darlene. His parents, Reverend Dr. Raymond Hampton, Jr. and Jacqueline Hampton, are extremely great role models in his life. They have extended their hands to many individuals and families that were destitute of daily needs, as well as became foster parents for many years to multiple children.

As a child and teenager, he was raised in Lynnwood, Washington where he attended elementary and high school. In July of 1991, at the age of twenty-six years old, he realized he had a passion to help people in a great way, so he went out on the street corner of Colby and Hewitt in Everett, Washington to start feeding the hungry and at that very moment, his outreach ministry was birthed with a folding card table, a ten-gallon McDonald juice container, ten loaves of bread and ten packages of Bologna.

He has now been consistent in doing community outreach for more than twenty-four years and currently is a pastor, author, outreach specialist, theologian, entrepreneur, philanthropist, television personality and public figure. He is known throughout the United States and Africa for his methodology and methods regarding outreach. His weekly television broadcast and hosting on Trinity Broadcasting Network/TBN entitled "Outreach with Ray Hampton" has inspired and motivated people from all walks of life, including the entertainment industry, business owners, executive directors, pastors, professional athletes to adults and children in the most deprived neighborhoods in the country. He has served as a Chaplain in a wide range of venues, such as the Snohomish County corrections facility to semi-pro soccer teams, as well as a mentor to many National Football League players from the Seattle Seahawks organization. He also believes in higher education, starting out at Washington State University and continuing his education at A.L. Hardy Academy of Theology. To his acclaim, he currently holds a Masters degree in Marriage and Biblical Family Counseling and two Doctoral degrees, one in Ministry and the other in Theology.

RAY HAMPTON has inspired thousands of homeless, helpless and hopeless individuals and families for over twenty-four years, not only by giving them a hand out, but a *hand up* through his many massive outreach giveaways, including over twenty-two thousand brand new toys at the annual "Christmas in the City Toy Giveaway" and to date, over sixty-eight thousand in total. In addition, over one hundred and seventy-two thousand meals have been prepared to feed the hungry on the streets of downtown Seattle's *Pioneer Square* and thousands of items of clothing, shoes and backpacks filled with school supplies. These are just a few of the major outreaches that have been used to impact many communities, cities and states. He lives in Seattle, Washington with his wife Julia, his high school sweetheart, whom he married at seventeen years old. They have been connected together not by contract, but by covenant, for over thirty-three years. Julia is extremely vital to his outreach success. Even though the calling on his life is great and rewarding, it is absolutely encouraging to know, according to the book Proverbs that it says, "He who finds a wife finds a good thing and obtains favor from the Lord."(Proverbs 18:22, ESV) In their thirty-three years of marriage, they have been blessed with five children in their union together: Trenecsia Nacol Bellinger, Raymond "Ramon" Hampton IV, Michael James Hampton, Catrena Sharde Hampton, Isaiah Cornelius Hampton and for twenty one years, have adopted and fostered multiple children, including Terrance Hampton, Tyrrell Hampton, Brittany Marie Hampton, Christian Franco, Hunter Franco and Brianna Franco. His calling in life is very simple, which is to find a need and fill it or a hurting heart and heal it and to provide an answer to a problem by serving with his palms down and not his palms up.

Contents

iREACH™

Bonus Material

IF YOU ARE AN OWNER of a business, a pastor of a church or a leader of a non-profit or for-profit organization and you want to increase your customer base, membership or partnership, this book is for you. Have you come to the conclusion that people are not fully paying attention to your memos, bulletins or newsletters, but instead focusing on their smart phone, iPad or tablet? As they are perusing through social networking sites such as email, Twitter, Facebook and many others, you realize there has to be a better way to communicate with you, while at the same time, remaining time conscious and financially accountable.

If you see yourself in one of these categories, I have some great news for you. This book that you're holding in your hand is loaded with methods I have personally used over the last twenty-five years to reach out to serve the rich and poor, both spiritually and physically. It is also used to empower and equip them, not only by giving handouts, but also a hand-up. You can have a competitive advantage over the next person simply by taking control of your time and not allowing distractions to deter you from your destiny by using digital and non-digital footprints.

iReach is not your ordinary book. It is a combination book/workbook that not only tells you what to do, but how to do it. You will learn how to use your favorite keywords to collect data from everyone you meet. Make one phone call and instantly be connected to thousands of people at the same time to get your message out or to have a live conversation. Text one message and tens of thousands of people will receive it in a matter of seconds. You will also have the capability to make your own digital flyers and mobile e-cards that will be sent out to as many people as you want, and receive a response back instantly. If you have a very busy schedule that makes it almost impossible to learn how to use multiple forms of software, pay multiple bills, scattering data across multiple platforms or even signing a contract, you have opened up the right book. *iReach* will teach you how to increase your value in partner-ship and how to use networking to enhance the value that has been added.

Inside, you will discover the following information:
- You cannot expand what you do not expose
- Think outside the box
- Work smarter not harder
- Your assignment is greater than your attack
- How to have an effective methodology and methods for outreach
- How you can have successful digital and non-digital outreach marketing
- The Four "P" Marketing Foundation
- Five Types of Outreach
- Potential Outreach Barriers
- Over Fifty Marketing Ideas
- Fundraising
- The Power of Partnership
- Keys to Networking

Chapter 1:
How to Market Your Outreach

BEFORE WE START TALKING about how to market your outreach, I want you to first retain in your knowledge what the two words marketing and outreach mean. Let's take a look at the word marketing. It is *the process involved in promoting, selling and distributing a product; the management process through which goods and services move from concept to customer.*

It includes the coordination of four elements, which are known as the four "P's" of marketing:

1. Identification, selection and development of a PRODUCT

2. Determination of its PRICE
3. Selection of a distribution channel to reach the customer's PLACE
4. Development and implementation of a PROMOTIONAL STRATEGY

Marketing is using your outreach program as a base to extend a hand, or uplift and fulfill a void in someone's life. Whenever you're using your outreach tools as marketing and not selling, you will always have a greater return, because you are teaching people how to fish and not just giving them a fish. This means they are not just being delivered from selling, but being developed through outreach marketing. Selling always comes with an idea and/or technique of getting someone to exchange cash for a product. The value of the product is not so much the issue.

Outreach marketing is developing and creating a demand to introduce a product and/or person to someone that may not feel valued. This helps them by supplying and fulfilling their needs not merely for a day, but for eternity.

Now that we have discussed marketing, I would like to explain to you why outreach marketing services are so important. The purpose for implementing a solid foundation for outreach is not just to be *affective*, but to be *effective*. Even though these words sound just alike, they actually have two very different meanings.

The root word for "affective" is "affect" and it's commonly used as an adjective, which means to influence an individual or group of people to make them feel, think or act in certain way. So, to be affective is one of the most important characteristics every outreach organization should possess to be successful in outreach marketing.

The root word for "effective" is "effect ". In contrast to the word affect, *effect* is used both as a noun and a verb. As a noun, the word effect generally means "the result of something". For something to be an effect, something else should have happened first. As a verb, it means: "the ability to produce the desired result" of the thing or person that is being affected. So, this is where all the confusion comes from in using the words *affective* and *effective* interchangeably.

Let's now bring these two words together, so you and/or your organization will not only be *affective*, but *effective* in all of your outreach marketing efforts. To be an affective person or organization means you have the ability to influence another person's feelings and way of thinking; causing them to act and feel a certain way. An effective person, on the other hand, is able to produce results without first influencing another person's emotions in order to produce desired results. Just because you are an affective speaker, does not mean that you are an effective outreach leader. Over the years, I have seen many great preachers that are affective behind the pulpit and their word delivery will have you jumping and shouting across the sanctuary. But in front of the pulpit and beyond the walls of brick and mortar, those same preachers are not very effective at all, because even though emotions were high inside the building, outside, no one was able to produce results.

Too many times, I have asked people leaving a church service, "What was the word today?" Their response was, "I don't know, but we sure did have some church today." There is a difference between having church and being the church. Having church is just the beginning, as it is working on your emotions to make you feel, think or act in a certain way, enabling you to receive what is being preached. It is affective, but there is more. Being the church is marrying it to your effectiveness, so that you can produce eternal results. When being affective is not connected to your effectiveness, it will always cause your organization to be ineffective. It will lack in power and the ability, or skill, to perform effective outreach marketing.

Let's get back to why outreach marketing is so important. One of the first reasons is because programs and giveaways can be done in very informal and differing types of settings. This will encourage more people to show up to events where there are different ethnicities, ages and belief systems. The people staffing the outreach are mainly, if not all, volunteers who serve their community, city and state, not because they have to do it in order to make a living, but because they are driven by their passion to give and not take. This type of person realizes that in order for them to live a successful life: spiritually, physically and financially, they must rely on the promise that was given to them from the foundations of the earth; delivered from their mother's womb. The day a spiritual transformation took place in your mind, you probably asked yourself this question, "What was I created to do on this earth?"

One thing I want you to always remember is that "the promise of prosperity is always connected to your passion." Now let's take a look at five different types of outreaches, including:

- PUBLIC RELATION'S OUTREACH
- DOMICILIARY OUTREACH
- DETACHED OUTREACH
- PERIPATETIC OUTREACH
- SATELLITE/DEDICATED SITE OUTREACH

1. PUBLIC RELATION'S OUTREACH: Public Relations is a form of outreach used to fill in the gap that mainstream services cannot offer. It provides an effective outreach program throughout the community, city and state. The majority of people would rather not give to an overhead expense, but will give to a program expense. They are vicariously able to touch more people through someone else and at the same time, their financial support has created a currency effect, as it continues to flow throughout the lives of thousands of individuals on the earth

2. DOMICILIARY OUTREACH: Provides care at someone's domicile; their permanent and legal residence and place of habitation. These individuals are unable to take care of themselves because of age or disability, and are in need of someone to assist them.

3. DETACHED OUTREACH: This type of outreach is performed in a public environment and provides services to disadvantaged individuals and families throughout the local community, city and state who would not normally receive the basic essentials for everyday living. These individuals can be in one of three categories, if not all, including being homeless, hopeless or helpless. For any organization to have a successful detached outreach program, it cannot be stationary. You have to be mobile and be willing to find the need and fill it. This cannot be done by waiting for them to come to you; you have to go to where they are.

4. PERIPATETIC OUTREACH: This type of outreach can be performed in public or private environments. It is different from detached outreach in that only certain individuals are targeted. Peripatetic outreach's purpose targets organizations only.

5. SATTELITE/DEDICATED SITE OUTREACH: Outreach services are dedicated to only one site, not multiple sites, such

as: apartment buildings, nursing homes, public or private schools, city parks, streets, parking lots or any similar place that is designated where your organization outreach can be effective.

POTENTIAL BARRIERS OF OUTREACH

The following key points could be potential barriers that could stop or slow down your outreach efforts, if you allow it to. If they are not discussed and implemented into your systems of operation within your organization, you will eventually become ineffective. This is not because it was not planted and prepared to grow, but because it was not properly watered and cultivated. In other words, there was no preparation before the elevation. Preparation is the action or process of making ready or being made ready for use or consideration, while elevation is the argumentation (the action or process of reasoning systematically in support of an idea, action or theory) of, or increase in the amount or level of something. So before your outreach can have increase, it first needs to be properly prepared mentally with practicum and people that are ready to serve.

Before we start talking about potential barriers, I need you to first understand the difference between methodology and methods. Methodology is the study of the method, or the description and explanation of the method, you use, but not the steps of carrying it out. It involves the learning of the various techniques that can be used, such as: your approach and perspective, how you will be studying a particular outreach concept.

Since Methodology explains the HOW, then what is the Method? The Method is defined as the WHAT, which are the steps you have to take in order to complete the assignment you have been given. Involved in your outreach methodology is a project methodology, which will provide the entire list of tasks for the outreach events and will allow the outreach director to modify any designated site assignments, depending on the location and type of outreach that is being offered. A work plan, which is a schedule that records and keeps track of all the organization's outreach projects that are accomplished throughout the year, will allow the organization to produce a method that will bring an active message of good news.

There are three questions I would like to ask you:"Do you have a vision? Do you have a mission? What is your organization's purpose? The word *vision* means having the ability to see ahead. Our organization's vision is very simple, "Each one, reach one." A mission is an assignment given to an individual or group. Our organization's mission is "To impact our city, our state and the world through outreach." The word purpose will always answer the question as to why your vision and mission are important. Our organization's purpose is "To empower and equip people all over the world to live a successful life." The following are a few things that could be barriers as to why your organization is not working effectively. I have also provided space for you to write down other barriers within your organization. You must be able to visualize it. You will never be able to conquer those things that you cannot confront.

OUTREACH BARRIERS THAT COULD BE AFFECTING YOUR ORGANIZATION

- Lacking clear goals
- Time management
- Passionate people
- Financial support
- Proper planning
- Partnership

- Consistency
- Networking
- Passion

- Persistence
- Productivity
- Produce

Write down a few of your own barriers not on the preceding list:

_____

_____

_____

_____

_____

_____

_____

CHAPTER ONE

HOW TO MARKET YOUR OUTREACH

1. What is the definition of the word marketing?

   _____

2. What is the definition of the word outreach?

   _____

3. What are the four "P's" of marketing?

- _____
- _____
- _____
- _____

4. What does the word affective mean?

_____

5. What does the word effective mean?

_____

6. Why is outreach marketing so important?

_____

7. What are the five different outreaches?

- _____
- _____
- _____
- _____
- _____

8. What is public relation outreach?

    _____

9. What is domiciliary outreach?

    _____

10. What is detached outreach?

    _____

11. What is peripatetic outreach?

    _____

12. What is satellite/dedicated site outreach?

    _____

13. What does preparation mean?

    _____

14. What does elevation mean?

    _____

15. What is the definition of the word methodology?

_____

16. What is the definition of the word method?

_____

17. What is the assignment of the individual who is in charge of pro-
    ject methodology?

_____

18. What is the assignment of an outreach director?

_____

19. What is the definition for the word vision?

_____

20. What is the definition for the word mission?

_____

21. Write down at least five outreach barriers that could be affecting
    your organization?

    • _____

- _____

- _____

- _____

- _____

Chapter 2:
Stay Motivated

THE CHURCH IS NOT JUST an organism that is growing, but it is also an organization. What is an organization? It is made up of distinct physical characteristics, including doors, windows, roof, etc. The floors of the building may be removed and replaced without destroying the integrity of the building but an organism cannot be treated in the same manner. The human body does not allow you to remove an eye, ear, arm, foot, fingernail or tooth without destroying the integrity of the body; without causing a mutilation to the body.

Your church, ministry or business needs to be marketed because of the great benefit it has to offer the community, which is providing help to disadvantaged individuals spiritually and physically. It's time for you to get out of your seat and on your feet and in the streets to start colliding with people. Throughout your community, city and state, there is a need for your services. You cannot just cause a collision in their life, but you must also be a great impact throughout their life. *Stop being just a hearer and a talker; become a doer. Why? Because someone is waiting for your obedience. Activate your assignment that you have been given for your life.*

If you continue to walk around trying to be everyone else, then who is going to be you? You are the only you that has ever existed and there has never been another you before you, and there will not be another you after you. So why would you try to be a copy when you are already the original? Have you ever asked God to bless an activity you were doing and it seemed like things were not coming together no matter how hard you were trying? Instead of stopping the activity, you kept on going, which consistently caused you to dig a hole of frustration within yourself. Inadvertently, it affected the people around you. *I wonder what would happen if you would stop asking God to bless what you are doing and start to do what He has already blessed.* Remember, He is not just moved by your needs; He is ultimately moved by your faith! Progress always precedes results.

SIX KEY PRINCIPLES TOWARD *EFFECTIVE* RESULTS

1. When you are quiet, you can listen effectively.
2. When you are listening effectively, you can remember.

3. When you are remembering, you will have a better understanding.

4. When your understanding is clear, you will always make good judgments.

5. When your judgment regarding a situation is understood, it is followed by your actions.

6. When your actions are activated, results follow.

Today is your day to stop looking like the "chosen frozen" and start to market the product you have been assigned to produce. Stop being distracted by the enemy and stop fighting over manmade denominations and dogmatic doctrines. Remember, the most important thing of all is to reach, teach and watch the transformation of an individual's life. Too much time is being spent discussing about denominations, doctrines and organization strategies, while tens of thousands of people are yelling for someone to come out and help. Even though our numerators might be different from one another, our denominator should be the same, which is to help people. In order to grow your church or business numerically, you have to be consistent in saturating the marketplace.

When a person decides they want to change the direction of their life from negative thinking to positive thinking, or if they just need help purchasing something, the first place they should think about receiving help is your organization. Let me ask you a question. What is the first thing that comes to your mind when you think about French fries and happy meals? Come on, let's say it together, "MCDONALDS," Even if you don't like the French fries at McDonald's, the organization has saturated your mind with their product through consistent advertising and outreach marketing. When you think about "happy meals", you will think "McDonald's".

Just like McDonald's presents their happy meals through outreach marketing, you, too, can do the same with your product and/or idea. If you are willing to be specific and consistent about your product/idea and if you would continue to cultivate what you have planted, you will soon see an increase within your organization as a result of your labor. The issue is never about a harvest, but always about the labor. Without labor, there will always be a problem throughout your organization, causing stagnation. Remember, marketing is not just designed to grow your organization, but ultimately, to expose your Church or business to greater spheres. What you don't expose will never expand. Every successful business in the world has a signature item or product and very knowledgeable salesmen that promote it, because they wholeheartedly believe in what they have been called to do. It amazes me how most, if not all, successful businesses start pushing their product first in their own community and city before they introduce it to the world. When it's done right, it will actually introduce itself, moving from outreach social marketing to attraction outreach marketing, which I will expand more upon toward the end of the book. If you would believe wholeheartedly in what you do and just start talking about the Good News and helping disadvantaged individuals spiritually and physically, your product will introduce itself to the world.

Remember, "You can never promote a product successfully without having passion for the product you are promoting."

BELIEVE-EXPECT-UNDERSTAND-TRUST

- You have to BELIEVE in the product you are offering because if you don't, who will?

- You have to EXPECT that something great is going to happen with the offering and acceptance of your product.
- You must understand the significance and value of your product and how it will help to propel another individual to their promotion and ultimately, their prosperity.
- You have to TRUST not just the creation, but the creator of the product.

For many years, people have been saying, "If you build it, they will come." There is some truth to this, but just because you build a big fish pond doesn't mean that all the fish are going to find their way to your pond, unless you go get them and lead and/or place them in the pond. Even though there are many great preachers across America that have grown "mega churches" with over eighteen hundred in weekly attendance, it is very important to remember that it is not the great preaching alone that grows mega churches. It is combined with "great leaders with focused leadership" that causes a church to become "mega". The question to be asked is, *"Can you, as a leader, connect the people within your organization to your assignment you have been given through vision casting?"* The reason why your vision is stagnating is because of the lack of connecting others to what you have been given to do.

Marketing is the key for growth in your church, ministry or business. Most people who struggle in this area will never see or live the life that has been laid out for them. Instead, they will always be frustrated with why they cannot live a passionate, purpose and fulfilled life. One of the main reasons you are not seeing the fulfillment of your life's vision is not because of the blueprint or foundation that has been made and dug for you, but because the enemy wants to steal, kill and destroy your destiny that God has planned for you. If someone breaks into your house, car or business, it seems like they should be happy and satisfied with just stealing your merchandise, but their ultimate goal is to kill your dreams that have been planted in your heart. If you are going to grow your organization, the first thing you must understand is that "Exposure always creates Expansion."

Can you imagine the tens of thousands of people that passed your location daily by walking, running or driving, but never knew that you existed? If your organization closes its doors today, would people know who you are? Would they know who used to be in that location and how you affected them? If they don't, then why? I have a very simple answer for you, you are not saturating your community, city and beyond with outreach marketing. That's why I have written and entitled this book *iReach*, which is simply the methodology of outreach provided to explain to you what your organization can do to get the word out to let everyone know why your organization exists.

Let's look at two groups of people, the first are the "irritators", which are "the chosen frozen" and the second group is known as the "motivators".

My question to you as a leader is which group do you represent? Would you like to represent the "chosen frozen" people who are not moving at all or would you like to represent the ones that have risen up out of their seats onto their feet and gone into the streets? This last group of people understands that in order for them to expand their organization, it is vitally important that they expose it to world.

THERE ARE FOUR TYPES OF PEOPLE IN THE WORLD:

1. There are people who WATCH things happen.

2. There are people who LET things happen.

3. There are people who ASK what happened.

4. There are people who MAKE things happen.

I personally decided that I did not just want to be a "watcher", an "enabler" or an "asker", but ultimately, I wanted to be a "maker" and allow the assignment I have been created for to flow out of me. To empower people to be the best they can be, by first feeding them physically and then, spiritually.

In July of 1991, we started our outreach organization to reach out to the homeless, hopeless and helpless. I quickly realized it would not be a great idea just to start preaching to the disadvantaged, since they were hungry, but rather give them something to eat and drink. As we met their physical needs, maybe they would listen to what we had to say? Ask yourself a question. Is your organization answering questions that nobody is asking, instead of answering questions that people are asking?

Make sure your outreach team is driven with the same passion and purpose that you have, because your inner-circle will either devalue your worth or raise your value. This is known as regression and progression. For instance, if there are twenty houses in a community and the nice home is surrounded by nineteen bad homes, the nice home is now devalued because of its surroundings. But if there are twenty houses in a community and the bad home is surrounded by nineteen nice homes, the property value of the bad home is raised because of being surrounded by so many nice homes. Never let anyone tell you that it does not matter who you spend your time with, because I'm here to let you know that bad company will always corrupt good manners. Just because it might seem permissible for you to hang around these types of individuals, it's probably not beneficial for you. In April of 1997, we formed a 501c3 organization known as *Seattle International Dream Center* and alongside of the dream center, we trademarked the name "Each One Reach One" and *"I-Reach,"* which are mobilization outreaches of the Dream Center.

The word EACH means everyone individually, or one by one. To REACH means to stretch or extend, as to touch or meet. Another definition would be to succeed in making contact with influencing, impressing, interesting or convincing. The word ONE means to be considered as a single unit or individual. To PRESENT something means to give, offer, represent or to act.

I'm going to ask you again, if your church or business closed down today, would people remember what was in that location or who you were? If you would like to have a great impact in your community or city, you first must have a "collision" with the people. The ultimate excitement does not end the first time people walk through the doors of your organization. That is the beginning, not the ending. It is when they come back through the door two, three, four or more times that should make you even more excited, because that means they are being empowered by what you have to offer. So two questions to ask yourself is, "How can I get people to come to my organization and how can I improve the retention process?" One thing vitally important to remember is that people never come uninvited.

AUTHORITY, ASSIGNMENT and ASSURANCE

Matthew tells the story of how Jesus gathered all of His disciples together that were with Him in the Garden before He died to commission them. These were the same disciples that watched Him walk on water, saw Him heal the sick, made the lame to walk and taught them how to pray.

What is the Great Commission?

The Great Commission is the instruction of the resurrected Jesus Christ to His disciples for them to be committed to spreading His teachings to all the nations of the world.

There is a limited Commission where the disciples were to restrict their mission to the Jews, to whom Jesus referred to as "the lost sheep of the house of Israel."

The most famous version of the Great Commission is in Matthew, where on a mountain in Galilee, Jesus calls on His followers to be baptized in the name of the Father, Son and the Holy Spirit and shared with them that the qualifications for making disciples is first being a disciple yourself. Even though everyone participates in different ways, we are still a valuable part of the mission and "No one is ever greater than their assignment."

When you know what your purpose and position is in Christ, no one but Jesus Christ Himself can disqualify you. People's criticism of your assignment should never bother you, because that is probably the only time they have ever thought about you. So stop worrying, being frustrated and trying to make them understand you. Your purpose did not come from them anyway. It was impregnated in you by the Holy Spirit, but needs to be cultivated and delivered by you. The assignment you were created for has never been done by anyone on this earth and that's why if you try to be someone else, then who is going to be you? So why don't you just DO YOU! Most people are satisfied just doing God's work and think they are completed in doing their assignment, but just because you're doing God's work does not mean you are doing God's assignment for your life.

"You will never be defeated by what other people say about you. You are only defeated by what you say about you. Have you ever stopped to wonder why every time you're getting close to or doing something great in your life, false accusations begin to arise around you through friends, family and/or business partners that you thought believed in you, as well as your product? If you have experienced this in your life, I have some great news for you; Never stop to answer your critics. Scandals only come out in the finals. Beware of people that smile at your defeats all the time, because a dog will always show his teeth when he gets ready to bite you. But the most important thing I want you to grasp through everything that I have spoken to you is in order to stay consistent in your outreach marketing efforts is to know that "failures are not final". Whenever people ask you how are you doing and your response is, "I'm just going through," turn it around with a positive tone, instead of a negative tone. The fact is, you are going through, but the truth is, to go through means that you are coming out. Now that's GREAT NEWS!

Most people are trying to continually chase their purpose, but actually their purpose is what pushes them into their destiny. That's why prayer is always the foundation and the key to your success, which will unlock the door of opportunity towards your destiny. If the door does not open, then it's not for you to walk through at that time. So just continue to rest in the Lord and trust that He knows the right time and He will give you peace that will surpass all your understanding.

This is why this book was written, to empower, encourage and enlighten you to stay mission-minded by reaching one person at a time. You can have all the plans you want for your life, but until you surrender your plans for the plan and purpose that has already been designed for you, you will never experience a fulfilling life. Remember, no one can stop God's plan for your life but you, so you might as well just DO YOU! Because, failure is never final.

CHAPTER TWO

STAY MOTIVATED

1. What is the definition of the word organization?

   _____

2. God is not just moved by your needs, He is ultimately moved by your _____.

3. Progress is always before _____.

4. What are the six key principles toward effective results?

- _____

- _____

- _____

- _____

- _____

- _____

5. The goal of outreach marketing is not only to grow the organization, but to _____.

6. What you do not _____will never expand.

7. You have to _____in the product that you are promoting.

8. You have to _____that something is going to happen.

9. You have to _____ the significance and value of your product.

10. You have to _____the creator of the product.

11. What is the key to growth for your organization?

_____

12. What are the four types of people?

- _____things happen.

- _____things happen.

- _____what happen.

- _____things happen

13. What does regression mean?

_____

14. What does progression mean?

_____

15. What does the word "each" represent?

_____

16. What does the word "one" represent?

_____

17. What does the word "reach" represent?

_____

18. What does the word "present" represent?

_____

19. No individual or group is greater than their _____.

20. Never stop your assignment to answer your _____.

21. Prayer is always the_____ and _____ to your organization's success.

Chapter 3
Marketing Strategies

DOES YOUR ORGANIZATION have a strong marketing outreach strategy?

It doesn't matter if you're a profit or non-profit organization; you are only effective when you have a strong marketing outreach strategy and are willing to be consistent and implement it. Your outreach marketing strategy does not have to be expensive to be effective. A major key in developing a marketing outreach strategy is to form a solid foundation to enhance your promotional efforts. Promotional efforts include, but are not limited to, advertising, mailing and/or phone calling. Not to have marketing outreach strategies is like buying a bunch of furniture for a home you're thinking about building, but you don't know what the square footage is. How would you even know how much furniture to buy or what size to buy?

TWENTY KEYS FOR OUTREACH MARKETING:

Key #1: You have to stay faith-focused.

Key #2: You cannot think any higher than the level you are exposed to, because exposure brings expansion.

Key #3: Your success is in your difference from others. What makes you unique from everyone else?

Key #4: What do you dislike that motivates you?

Key #5: Don't expect everyone to understand you, because there has never been another you before you existed.

Key #6: Practice not only gives you perfect results, but it will also give you permanent results.

Key #7: Competition is never against someone else; it's only against yourself to be the best you.

Key #8: If you try to be someone else, then who is supposed to be you?

Key #9: What are you good at that will maximize your potential?

Key #10: You have to be in tune to the sound and rhythm of your assignment and calling for your life.

Key #11: Change is only change when you change.

Key #12: Preach the Gospel and if necessary, use words.

Key #13: Don't try to change the world, but change your world.

Key #14: Look for problems in your community where you can provide an answer.

Key #15: Always serve with your palms down and not your palms up.

Key #16: Don't live your life "tapping" people, but live your life "touching" people.

Key #17: People don't care how much you know, until they know how much you care.

Key #18: What is your competitive advantage?

Key #19: Know your identity.

Key #20: Reach the "ONE".

There are many non-profit and for profit organizations trying to reach the thousands, but they always miss the "one" failing to realize by reaching the "one", they will eventually touch the thousands. Again, this is what I have often heard my son refer to as "Process over Results". In the Fall of 2014, I recall when Raymond Hampton IV (aka: Ramon) who is my oldest son, took his family on a hiking trip to climb Tiger Mountain. His wife Lindsay had just recently delivered a baby. She was only five months old. With baby Sasha strapped tightly to her mother's body, she carried her up the mountain.

Leading the pathway was her six-year-old son, Raymond Hampton V (aka: Rai or Cinco) walking in front of his dad. Of course his dad kept a good eye on him as he was still in arm's reach, but Rai was the man leading the team. As you can see from the timeframe of the writing of this book, there are five generations of Raymond's and we are all still alive and well. Now this is really known as outreach marketing, if you know what I mean. One thing I remembered my son explaining to me was that he said, "Dad it took us around three hours to get to the top of Tiger Mountain and as we were going up to the top, a lot of people had given up, turned around and started to go back down the mountain. But we stayed through the process, because we wanted to finish what we started. There are many times in life that your own strength will not accomplish your assignment or assignments, but it is through Christ who gives you the ultimate strength to accomplish the assignment you have been assigned to do. Remember, since He began the work in you, He will see that it's completed through you. If you continue to stay with Him, the rewards are great and the daily benefits are loaded with blessing.

As they were climbing Tiger Mountain, they stayed faith-focused on the "process", which was, "A series of actions or steps taken in order to achieve a particular end" and the higher they went up, the thinner the air became, but that did not stop his family from climbing. Why? Because there was an end goal to be achieved: to make it to the top. Once his family arrived to the top of Tiger Mountain, he shared with me that when he looked down the mountain to see all the cars and things below, to his amazement, he could see, but he could not hear any of the sounds. Sometimes in life, you need to ignore the distractions, or sounds, around you which will allow you to only hear the voice of God's direction for your life. When He is not speaking, it is a good idea for you not to make a move at all and just continue to rest in Him. To rest does not mean for you to completely stop what you're doing, but it does mean for you to continue what you are currently doing, until He gives you the green light to move forward.

Promotion does not come merely from what you are doing; it is received by what He is doing through you. I have shared with tens of thousands of people throughout the years that success means to "follow the instructions that you have been given to do without asking a bunch of details." I have spent a lot personal time and money throughout my life trying to find someone that was doing effective outreach just like what was planted in my heart to do. There were organizations that were similar, but not the same. I kept running into a dead end street trying to find the assignment that was exactly like what was planted in my heart to do. As I search and served, I was never fulfilled only "filled", but not "full", so I just did whatever they did. Not that it was the wrong thing to do, but ultimately, it was just not the right thing for me to do. Just because all things might be permissible to you does not mean they are beneficial for you. One day, something just landed in my thought process and I came to the realization that "If I kept trying to be everybody else, then who was going to be me" and "maybe what I was created for had not even been invented yet." So, I just activated my measure of faith and did what I was created to do. Since I had already been delivered from a negative way of thinking, I definitely did not want to go back there again, because I now realized that whatever and however an individual thinks, they will possibly become. I stopped depending upon my own knowledge and started to trust the One that not only gave me knowledge, but who can also, at anytime, enhance the knowledge He has already given me. Once I started to listen and carry out my assignment throughout the nation, that's when all the attacks began on and in my life. As always, I went to the source who is the provider of all resources, where there was always a comforting word. I knew, at that moment, that my assignment was greater than the attacks that were trying to distract me and as long as I stayed in my lane, I would never get into a wreck. There might be people in front of me that are going faster or people behind me pushing me, but as long as I stay in my lane, I knew I would continue to move forward in the plan, path, promises and prosperity for my life, because I was committed to pushing toward my destiny.

COMPLETING VS COMPETING

The assignment you have been assigned to for your life is not to compete against another individual, but to complete them. You are not supposed to be in competition with others, but only to encourage, empower or to be in covenant with others, especially when it comes to the outreach marketing of your organization. I will be expounding more on this subject within the chapters on "partnerships" and "networking".

At 11:00pm one evening in 1991, as I was watching the news and hearing so much about people who were living on the streets that were homeless and hungry, something within me was stirring up and at that very moment, I knew that I was called to make a difference in another person's life through serving. To do this effectively, I knew that I could not change the whole world, but I could change my world, and once my world was changed, everything that I was connected to would begin to change. After days, weeks and months went by; I continued to watch the news regarding the issues of the homeless and the hungry. It continued to rise at an alarming rate and suddenly one day, the sounds of bells began to go off in my spirit. At that very moment, I knew it was time to sound the alarm. I began to feel a shift within my spirit to do something great in my life by being a solution to the problems that had arisen concerning the homeless and hungry by providing an answer to the need.

There are probably many times throughout your life that you may have had a good idea, but it might not necessarily have been a God idea. Do you know what the difference is between a GOOD IDEA and a GOD IDEA? Good ideas are God's permissive will, but God ideas are God's perfect will for your life. I definitely wanted to be in the perfect will of God. I didn't have a Bachelor's degree, a Master's degree, or a Doctoral degree, but I began to search the Word of God for faith scriptures that pertained to what had been stirred in my heart and on my mind. At that moment, I realized that since I had been born again, I actually had my Bachelor's degree and since I had been touched by the Master, I had my Masters degree and last but not least, I had a PhD, because I had the power of the Holy Spirit and had been delivered. So, if I just continued to trust in the Lord with all my heart and lean not to my own understanding and acknowledge Him, He would direct all of my steps. Even though, at times, I may have stumbled, I was still stepping.

The great news is at the time of this writing, I have accomplished the goal of my continual higher educational success by attending Washington State University and A.L. Hardy Academy of Theology where I received my Bachelors in Theology, Masters in Marriage and Family Counseling and two doctoral degrees, the first one is a Doctorate in Ministry (D.Min) and the second is a Doctorate in Theology (Th.D).

The purpose for profit and non-profit organization advertisement is not for you to know who they are. If I were to ask you if you have ever heard of McDonald's, Wendy's, Burger King, Kentucky Fried Chicken, Jack-in-the-Box, Taco Bell, Taco Time, White Castle, Crystals, Cracker Barrel, Ryan's, Old Country Buffet, Golden Corral, Microsoft or Amazon, my guess is that you have heard of at least one of these organizations, if not all. But none of these companies have to advertise with signage on the building or property for you to "know who they are". Advertisement is so you "don't forget who they are".

Nike and Verizon don't advertise because you do not know who they are. Their goal is to convince you that going to any other company to buy products will not be of the same value. These companies create a mental awareness to make you think about a product that someone else sells that is similar to theirs. You will always go to them, because of their marketing strategy. They have implanted a thought in your mind to think that their value of the product is always higher than everyone else's. This term is known as "competitive advantage". Competitive advantage is a condition or circumstance that puts a company in a favorable or superior business position and expansion is vital to maintaining a competitive advantage.

As an organization, if your continued focus would be on building people, instead of building buildings, you would not have a building big enough to contain all the people you have empowered and equipped. Full capacity in your building would mean that you would have to call for help to share in the harvest. This is what I call "People over Product".

When companies realize that their sales are down, one of the first things they do is increase their marketing spending for the next quarter.

They understand that in order for revenue to increase, they must expose their problem for deeper penetration in the market. When your profit or non-profit organization is in a financial bind, the very first thing most leaders do is delete some, if not all, advertisements from the outreach marketing budget. The very thing that is helping to expose the organization has now been deleted from the budget. They continue to fund programs that are stagnant, instead of realizing without people there are no programs. To help you with this process, I have compiled tools to give you a jumpstart in the following chapter. In order for you to have a successful outreach marketing organization, you need to be utilizing digital and non-digital footprints for all of your outreach marketing ideas.

CHAPTER THREE

MARKETING STRATEGIES

1. Your outreach marketing strategy does not have to be _____ to be _____.

2. What is the major key in developing an outreach marketing strategy?
   _____.

3. What are three examples of promotional efforts, but not limited to?

   • _____

- _____

- _____

4. What are the twenty keys for outreach marketing?

    - You have to stay _____ _____.
    - You can't think any higher than the level that you are ex-
      posed to because _____ brings _____.

    - Your success is in your _____from others what makes
      you _____ from everyone else.

    - What do you dislike that _____you?

    - Don't expect everyone to _____you because there has nev-
      er been another *you* before *you* existed.

    - Practice not only gives you _____results, but it will give you
      _____results.

    - _____is never give someone else is only get yourself
      to be the best you.

    - If you try to be someone else, then who is supposed to be
      _____?

    - What are you good at that will _____your _____?

- You have to be in tune to the _____ and _____ of your assignment and calling for your life.

- Change is only _____ when you _____.

- Preach the _____ and if necessary use _____.

- Don't try to change the _____, but change your _____.
- Look for _____ in your community where you can provide an _____.

- Always serve with your _____ _____ and not with your _____ _____.

- Don't live your life _____ people, but live your life _____ people.

- People don't _____ how much you know until they know how much you _____.

- What is your _____ advantage?

- Know your _____.

- Reach the "_____".

5. _____ is always over _____.

6. What is the definition of the word process?

_____

_____

7. What is a "Good" idea? _____

8. What with a "God" idea? _____

9. What is the purpose of advertisement for non-profit and for profit organizations?

_____

10. What does the term "competitive advantage" mean?

_____

_____

11. The main purpose of an outreach organization is to _____ people not _____.

12. When you are people focused instead of product focused, it is called "_____ over _____".

13. Without people there are no _____.

Chapter 4

What is Digital and Non-Digital Footprint Marketing?

A DIGITAL FOOTPRINT IS the data left behind by users on digital services. There are two main classifications for digital footprints: passive and active. A passive digital footprint is created when data is collected without the owner knowing, whereas active digital footprints are created when personal data is released deliberately by a user for the purpose of sharing information about oneself by means of websites and/or social media.

A non-digital footprint is just the opposite; it is not using the web at all, but it is your hand extended to someone else, physically and not just electronically. This type of marketing is known as traditional marketing, because there is a paper trail of events that have been captured by word of mouth.

The following ideas are given for you to "think outside the box". I truly believe that God did not intend for you to be, or remain, in a box. Neither did He want you to be more concerned about church work than Kingdom work. Church work might be a "good idea", but Kingdom work is a "GOD idea. What is the major difference between these ideas? A "good idea" is from yourself and the encouragement of other people that are connected to you or those around you. But a "GOD idea" is when God gives you a revelation that only He can reveal. If you refuse to accept and move on it, you will miss the manifestation that God has for your life. Many people have gone out to do Kingdom work to try to increase their weekly attendance, but when they did not see the increase, they stopped everything they were doing; failing to realize that Kingdom work takes a while to grow. Just because you don't see it right away, does not mean it is not working. It is not the one that does the planting or watering who is at the center of this process; it is God who makes all things grow.

FIFTY-TWO OUTREACH MARKETING IDEAS THAT WILL INCREASE YOUR NUMBERS WITHIN ONE YEAR BY SIMPLY DOING ONE A WEEK.

ARE YOU READY TO START NOW?

READY...SET...GO!

1. HANDOUTS- Door hangers, fliers and postcards: your 5 x 7 postcards should be out of the envelope and mail ready with return address already printed on them so post office workers, can see them. As your invitation or announcement travels to its destination, it should be exceptional and attractive. When getting your postcard printed, use a glossy card stock and if you want the front of your card to really shine for extra money, you can have a UV coating placed on it, though not necessary. Just make sure you DO NOT put UV coating on the back of the card (this is where the return address and stamp is located) because once it is at the post office and being processed, the meter strip ink at the bottom of the card will smear and not stick to the card. Also, when the information is printed on this side of the card, leave an open space one inch from the bottom with no writing in this area. This is where the mailing label will be and also so the machine will not detect any unnecessary writing that it thinks is the address.

2. BILLBOARDS- Billboards are great advertisements; once you find a heavy traffic area or an area you would like to saturate, you have just taken your first step toward community and city-wide outreach marketing. Now, the second step is to notice that on each billboard sign, there is a number on it which will help you with your conversation when calling the agency. Once you call the agency, give them that number and/or street location and you are now ready for outreach marketing by attracting the people in the city. They will now be looking for you, instead of you looking for them. The question you might still be wondering is why you should use billboards for advertising your organization? The answer is simple. Because everyone sees it!

3. BUS STOPS- Bus stops are a great means of outreach marketing to the entire Community. People are already traveling throughout the

city and as they are waiting for their bus to arrive, they are also looking at your advertisement. Your organization is consistently on their mind throughout the day. Just think about the tens of thousands of people that are riding on the city transit or metro buses with your name implanted in their mind. If only a half-percent show up at your organization, it's worth the marketing.

4. GROCERY STORE SHOPPING CARTS- Everyone goes shopping and every time they place food in their shopping cart, they are looking at your advertisement. This advertisement is always placed on the inside or the outside nose of the shopping cart. I have been amazed by the amount of requests and/or donations I have received because of our advertisement that said,"$1.00 a day will keep hunger away". Keep it simple, but effective so you can get the results you're expecting.

5. RADIO-AM- stations are not bad; they just have weaker signal strength than FM. Most people listen to popular stations on FM, so this is where you should do your advertisement or broadcast. Depending upon your target audience, make sure that your advertisement is relevant to the listeners that you seek to reach. For example, if you want the young Rhythm & Blues listeners, ask the station for a printout of their listening audience.

6. MOVIE THEATERS- can you imagine eight movie screens in a theater that show four movies a day showing your advertisement? That means your product and/or idea is shown thirty-two times a day, seen by captivated thousands of people while they eat popcorn, hotdogs and drink soda. This is called network marketing by attraction. You are building the first step of network marketing without even being there.

7. FAMILY AND FRIENDS DAY- on this "BIG" day you can have everyone dress casual or wear a t-shirt with your organization's name on it or the theme for that day. Every member is encouraged to invite at least one guest and share with them that there will be multiple drawings and food served. There are multiple drawings of gift certificates to local businesses and special musical selections. Great ideas for giveaways are T.V.'s, vacation packages, grocery store certificates, dinner for one, two or for the entire family at their favorite restaurant, Xbox, Play Station, bikes and more. On family and friends day, the greatest asset in your organization is the members of your organization. Family and friends day should be done at least four times a year. If scheduled more than four times during the year, it will lose its excitement.

8. TEXTING- statics shows that over 55% of the nation has a smart phone. You can communicate effectively using your cell phone by using a mobile texting app like TEXT NOW, which allows free texting from a number you set up on your own not connected to your cell phone number, but located on your Smartphone or tablet. You can also use a mass texting service such as CLUBTEXTING.COM or EZTEXTING.COM.

9. EMAILING- statistics also show that emailing is a very effective tool that everyone can receive on their computer, iPad or Smartphone. Giving an individual a key word and a text number, you can have them immediately added onto your mass email list at your office. The days of writing it down on paper and losing or forgetting it before you arrive to your office is over. This can be done by using mass email services, such as: CONSTANTCONTACT.COM or MAILCHIMP.COM.

10. PHONE CALLING- The days of calling one person at a time is over. Can you imagine having to call everyone that you meet throughout the day and week to remind them of upcoming events that you're having? There is not enough time in the day for you to accomplish this task effectively. There is a way that "one phone call will do it all", instead of trying to reach the thousand and miss the one. Now, by reaching one, you can connect to thousands for approximately five cents a call or five dollars to reach one hundred people. It will only take you ninety seconds to do. This can be accomplished by using a service called: SIMPLEBLAST.COM.

Are you looking for someone's name, phone or address that you haven't seen in years? All you need is one of the three to locate them today anywhere in the United States by going to SPOKEO.COM and paying a very small fee as you get to enjoy your search and connect with family and friends across the United States.

11. FACEBOOK- you can create a Facebook group for your organization and send them an invite by doing the following steps:

1. Go to FACEBOOK.COM and create a "like" page for your organization.
2. Solicit twenty-five "likes" so that you can establish a "vanity url" for your "like" page.
3. Launch a group and keep it locked.
4. Send an "inbox" invite to join the group to your new members using their Facebook address.
5. Post a welcome message in the locked group welcoming each new member once they have accepted the invite.
6. Email within seventy-two hours of the new member joining.

12. VIDEOS ONLINE- You can create a YouTube or Vimeo account and keep recorded events online where anyone can watch. Upload and share videos twenty-four hours a day, which will expand the exposure of your organization. It's very important to remember: "What you do not expose will never expand". This can be done by using the following steps:

1. Go to YouTube.com and establish an account.
2. Upload three videos to change the status of your account to a channel.
3. You can record "welcome" or "thank you" videos to individuals you have connected with and after giving a general message, you can have the editor roll across the lower third of the video the names you would like to highlight. You can also make this video private and email it to individuals or just keep it open to the public.
4. Record and upload every major event that you do in order to gain exposure for your organization.

Or You Can:

1. Go to Vimeo.com and establish an account.
2. Upload three videos to change the status of your account to a channel.
3. You can record "welcome" or "thank you" videos to individuals you have connected with and after giving a general message, you can have the editor roll across the lower third of the video the names you would like to highlight. You can also make this video private and email it to individuals or just keep it open to the public.

4. Record and upload every major event that you do in order to gain exposure for your organization.

13. TWITTER- Twitter is another effective way of communicating with people that have Smartphones. You can connect with thousands of people by using their Twitter name, such as:@drrayhampton. Go to TWITTER.COM to set up your account today.

14. INSTAGRAM - What's this thing called "Instagram" that everyone is talking about? Instagram is a social networking app made for sharing photos and videos from a Smartphone. Similar to Facebook or Twitter, everyone who creates an account has a profile and news feed. When you post a photo or video on Instagram, it will be displayed on your profile. Other users who follow you will see your posts in their own feed. Likewise, you'll see posts from other users who you choose to follow. Set up a Instagram account for your organization and you can keep it private or public and use it to post pictures from special events. If your account is kept private, only your members can view it. Get all of your outreach marketing out TODAY by going to INSTAGRAM.COM.

15. CONFERENCE CALL- instead of one on one calling, call waiting or three-way Calling, how about using your same phone to talk to between100 to 1000 people at one time. You will be able to have the capability of engaging in a conversation not just with one individual, but multiple individuals. You can be the teacher and they can be the students, as they are even able to respond to your questions where everyone can hear. At the end of the lesson, you can open the conversation up for individual questions by explaining to your students, members or business associates on number demands they are able to push on their phone. You can also record the conversation so anyone can come back as many

times as they want to listen to what has been communicated. I remember one time receiving a lot of snow in Seattle and no one was able to attend church so instead, we had online church by using SIMPLEBLAST.COM for the phone calling, CONSTANTCONTACT.COM for emailing and CLUBTEXTING.COM for texting to let everyone know to call in to a certain number at certain time that would connect us all together. After the conversation was over, people were then directed to the website to give their financial contribution through PayPal to whatever outreach event we were doing at the time. The following three steps will introduce you to a new way of conducting your meetings by doing online meetings in times of emergency or non-emergency:

1. You will be given a call in number.
2. A backup number.
3. A recorded message number.
4. A host participant code.
5. A participant code.

You can even have the capability of sending your recorded meeting by email to anyone you would like by downloading it onto your computer.

This is a FREE service and all you need to do is go online to FREECONFERENCING.COM and start growing your organization today!

16. CD MESSAGE- Do you record your messages on a CD at your church and/or business? Would you like to get that message recorded to individuals quickly and effectively without waiting for them to purchase

the CD because there is important information you would like them to have NOW?

1. Set up an account on SOUNDCLOUD.COM.
2. Upload your important message.
3. Email each individual the audio recording of your message as an MP3 file.
4. Email this within 72 hours for new members joining.

17. WEBSITE- The importance of having a website is to keep everyone informed across the United States and internationally about updates of your organization. There are three things that are very important in keeping your website informative. You must have a mission statement, vision statement and purpose of your core values and philosophy. Your organizational structure plan needs to be simple with clarity, but effective. Do not use Gmail, Hotmail, etc. for email addresses if possible. Always have your email address match your website, because people sometimes do not take you serious when they don't. They will not take you seriously. You can build your own website for free by going to a free website builder, such as WIX.COM or any other free sites. You can have it professionally created by going to CHEVYCORTEZ.COM or other professional sites and then go to GODADDY.COM, so they will be able to host it for a small fee, depending on how long you want them to host. They also will provide you with a certain amount of emails that are free that will be conformed to your website. GODADDY will also provide the domain name for you as well. Remember, when everything matches, it gives your organization a professional look!

18. BOOKS- writing your own book or manual is another great marketing tool to use when trying to get your point across. It allows you to get your plans, visions and dreams out of your head and onto paper. You don't have to spend thousands of dollars to create your book. All you need to do is:

1. Write it
2. Type it
3. Have it edited
4. Upload your manuscript to the publisher's website.

If you don't feel like you have the writing skills but you like to talk, you can create an audio book. If you don't want to be responsible for handling paper or hardback books, you can create an eBook, or why not create all three? It doesn't matter how you do it, just do something.

The following companies can produce a professional looking book for you. You can buy one, two, three or many as you want at a time and your books will be ready for you to sell. The following publishing companies are just a few to get your pen, paper, tablet and/or computer ready to take the information knowledge in your head and into your first manuscript. Now, what are you waiting for? No excuse now! The pen will not work, unless you pick it up and guide it.

- INSTANTPUBLISHER.COM
- CREATSPACE.COM
- HUNTERHEARTPUBLISHING.COM

19. PHONE APP- phone apps are another great tool, because every-one that has a Smartphone uses phone apps. Phone apps can give an individual all the information that you want them to know about your

organization. All they would need to do is download your app to their phone and once they receive your app, they can be up to date about your upcoming outreach events.

The following are just two impactful ways a mobile app can add immediate value to your organization:

1. You can increase your visibility by millions. Most organizations experience more downloads than people within their organization, which will not only cause growth of outside exposure, but expansion inside, as well.

2. You can receive a significant increase in your daily financial contributions by having an easily accessible place for anyone to give through their phone app, such companies like CHURCHAPP.COM, SUBSPLASH.COM or APPMAKR.COM, highly recommend.

The following are nine productivity apps that you can download for free to increase your outreach marketing:

• Dropbox|Cloud storage, File Sharing

Dropbox offers secure content sharing. It makes it easy to access and edit your files, share content, and stay connected with your team from anywhere on any device. Share important files with your staff, keep your presentation at your fingertips, comment on documents on the go, and view updates to your spreadsheets instantly. A lot of people use Dropbox for storage of personal files, such as family photos, important documents, etc. It is not normally used for a profit or non-profit organization. Dropbox will allow you and your team to work more efficiently and stay connected. Dropbox recently added the ability to edit Microsoft office documents on your mobile phone. If you want to make an update to a Word or Excel document, just pull it up in Dropbox and you now have the option to make changes right on your phone! This document will open in Word or Excel, so you'll need to have those free apps installed also.

- PayPal and PayPal Here|Finance, Mobile Payments

PayPal is a popular financial service that can be used to make payments, receive Payments, or even just send money to a friend or family member. If you have an online business, you probably already accept PayPal as a method of payment. You can even use PayPal to take payments in person and send your customer a receipt through text or email.

- Over|Photo Editing

Instagram is a fast growing, photo sharing, digital media platform. It is an extremely effective marketing platform that is overlooked by many non-profit and for profit organizations. When you're using Instagram for your outreach marketing and advertising, you will often want to add text to your images. There are many apps that will allow you to do this, but OVER is one of the best. You get control over where the text appears, the size, color and effects, and several fonts to choose from. OVER saves you the time and hassle of importing your image to your computer, modifying it in the photo-editing or graphic design software, and exporting it back to your phone. Some of your most effective ads and posts will be created right in the palm of your hands on your Smartphone.

- Evernote|Note-Taking/Organization

Evernote will keep your thoughts, research and projects organized for you. If you are a person that keeps a binder for every major project that you work on, which contains all of your personal notes, tear sheets, reference articles and images, Evernote is like a digital version of all of your binders in one place. In other words, it's an "all in one binder".

- Expensify|Finance, Expense Tracking

Expensify makes capturing receipts, tracking time or mileage, business travels and creating expense reports quick and easy. It is generally regarded as the best app for expense reporting. Expensify takes the time and paper out of your expense reports! Use Expensify to take a picture of your receipt,then select which report the expense goes on, and you're done. Smart scan technology reads the receipt and creates the expense, eliminating manual entry and saving you valuable time. If you are the CEO/President/Manager/Pastor/Director of a small, medium or large-sized Non-profit or for profit organization, you can use Expensify, so you don't need to have an accountant on staff, but it's always good to consult a CPA regularly.

- Genius Fax|Fax PDF Documents

You don't have to rush anymore to your local copy center or pay ridiculous prices just to fax one page when you can let Genius fax do all the work for you.

- Genius Scan|Mobile Scanning

Genius scan is a quick and easy solution when you don't have immediate access to a scanner. It enables you to quickly scan documents on the go and email the scans JPEG or PDF with multiple pages. In addition, you can unlock the Genius scan+ features, which allow you to export your scans wherever you want: box, Dropbox and other Cloud service apps installed on your phone that support JPEG or PDF files. The Genius scan scanner technology includes smart page detection, perspective correction an image post processing. Basically, you can take a picture of a page and the app makes it look like you scanned it on a professional scanner! Another great feature is that documents, or processes it, on your phone and is not sent to a third party server.

- Google Analytics|Website Traffic Monitoring

It can be very difficult to find time to get into your Google Analytics and see, in detail, how your site is doing. It is important to keep track of where your traffic comes from, what's popular on your site, and what is not, as well as who is visiting your page. Google recently released a mobile app so you can check all of these items and it does not matter where you are located! You can always check your website traffic on the go, which would enable you and/or your team to make changes in real-time to maximize your website's performance.

- Signed Documents

Are you having problems connecting with your customer to sign papers? Well, I have great news for you; your worries are over! Turn on your Smartphone, download the DocuSign app and get started today by getting and/or receiving signatures electronically, or go to:

❖ DOCUSIGN.COM.

❖

There are so many apps that are available on the market today and growing daily that it would be impossible for me to list and keep up with all of them in this iReach book. If you know of any that will enhance outreach marketing, please email me at:

❖ RayHampton@EachOneReachOne.net

20. FUNDRAISING- It's time to put the word "FUN" back into FUNdraising by having a successful mail or online department within your organization, as non-profit organization donations are very important for the life of the organization. Over 95% of every non-profit in the United States accept donations through email and other social media technology. I would like to ask you two important questions: Are you offering a way for people to donate online? Are you making it easy for people to make donations from their mobile device?

The average non-profit organization is either doing one or neither. I would like to show you three endeavors to increase your fundraising campaign, such as: how to put together a plan to let your supporters know about your campaign, why they should donate to your organization, how to execute your plan, and how you can extend your organizational structure plan to have continued success throughout the year. All you would need to do to have an effective structure for outreach marketing is an online donation page, email list of supporters with their permission, and a Facebook page for the organization.

HOW TO PLAN YOUR DONATION CAMPAIGN

Before your organization begins their donation campaign, the planning strategy will be a very important foundation in getting it from the runway to take off and to its destination, which means getting it in front of the right people. The following is the four step process to arrive to your destination. What is the definition of the word STEP? It is a series of actions, processes, or measures taken to achieve a goal. Outreach marketing can be described as using a specific message to communicate between your group and the public for mutual benefit. This step-by-step process is intended to be used as a tool to help you create your own outreach FUNdraising strategy plan.

STEP #1. Setting your goals.

Your goals should be unique to your organization and your general statements should express a broad outreach focus. The goals and statements may include the increase of staff, paid or volunteers, as well as building community recognition. Your objectives should be specific and measurable, such as increasing volunteers, outreaches or more financial support by 20% in the next six months. What's your vision of success? Of course you want people to donate, but after the campaign has ended, what specifically would make it a success? What is the dollar amount? What will these funds enable you to do that you're currently not able to get done?

- Write down your goals:

_____

_____

_____

_____

_____

STEP #2. Understand your target group.

Your target audience is the group of people you want to reach.

Some criteria for defining your target audience may include age, parental status, ethnicity, homelessness, etc. Your mission statement will be very helpful in focusing on the target groups of people you want to reach. Keep in mind that not everyone has access to the same things. The key is to meet each target group where they are socially and economically. Different methods will always attract different people, but will have the same message.

Lower-income people often do not have access to the internet, so you would need to place flyers where lower income and/or urban parents spend time, such as a Laundromats, parks etc. Remember, it is the "message" that is sacred, not the "method". Always make sure you provide a way for your target audience to receive additional information; through a telephone number, website, or meeting time/place. Again, remember that not everyone may have access to a telephone or computer.

Once you have thought about what you want to accomplish, you can shift your focus to the people you're trying to reach and a great place to start is with your supporters that have been financially giving consistently daily, weekly, monthly or even annually.

- Write down your answers:

Why do your biggest supporters support your organization?

_____

_____

_____

_____

_____

What is unique about the work that you're doing?

_____

_____

_____

_____

_____

_____

What has inspired your supporters to donate to your organization in the past?

_____

_____

_____

_____

_____

_____

Was there a particular fundraiser that exceeded your expectations?

_____

_____

_____

_____

_____

_____

What is the average amount your supporters generally give annually, monthly or even daily? (Write down a financial a range.)

_____

_____

_____

_____

STEP #3. Understanding your value.

Your supporters have many organizations they can financially support. Why should they support your organization?

_____

_____

_____

_____

_____

_____

Who will benefit from the financial support of your supporters?

_____

_____

_____

_____

_____

_____

Why is your organization asking for financial support?

_____

_____

_____

STEP #4. How to package your method and deliver your message.

Now that you have a targeted group, you can assess the target group and create the message. Now, it's time to determine the best delivery of your organization's message that has been packaged. Packaging can have many forms, including flyers, a script using a phone tree or an advertisement in a local paper. Brainstorm with the rest of your team about what form you want your message to take. Always keep in mind the resources that you may already have available in front of you. For example, someone in the group may work at a place that will provide discounts for photocopying, etc. Once you have decided what format will be best, decide as a team how to best prepare your message and method to get it out effectively. Remember to always set deadlines for each task to be completed, because it is not real until you write it down, so start now.

STEP #5. Creating your financial support campaign.

How to create your FUNdraising campaign.

To create a successful fundraising campaign, you will be using steps 1-3. Step number one, which is setting your goals, is one of the most important steps of creating your donations page. You will then use steps two and three to start drafting your organization's donation campaign.

Your financial supporters have many other organizations that they can support, so why should they support your cause? Who will be benefiting from the financial support that you have been able to raise from your organization?

If your organization wanted to raise $5000.00 to provide gifts for children during Christmas, in order to do this successfully, you would first need to know the average donation from each of your financial supporters. Then, you will also have to show your supporters how their funds will be used, because they are more likely to donate if they know the cause that they are financially supporting and the percentage toward the cause. Once you know your financial goal amount and what your average financial supporter gives, then you can ask for a suggested donation of the average amount to meet your goal, based on the amount of people on your list.

By evaluating your outreach plan at the end of each event, you can determine what worked or did not work, and what adjustments need to be made for the future. There are many different tools to work your plan. Some messages will have obvious ways to measure results. For example, if you used the outreach plan to organize a winter coat drive, the number of coats you got back is an evident way to determine how successful you were, and so on. Meet with your team about how your results compared to your goal, how did they think people responded to your message and method, and what needs to be changed to make it more effective next time.

The days of being stressful and the straining of raising funds are over. It's time for you to put the word "FUN" back in FUNdraising, so you can "work smarter and not harder" by raising the funds you need for your project online. While you're sleeping, people are giving online twenty-four hours a day toward your cause. The following companies can help you with raising thousands of dollars:

- CROWDFUNDING.COM
- SNAP-FUNDRASING.COM
- GOFUNDME.COM

22. TRADEMARK- trade marking your item will protect anyone from using your name in the state where you live. You can also have your item federally trademarked, which will protect it within the United States. In either case, if someone uses your trademarked item, they have to legally pay you for your hard work that you have done. It does not matter if they have been saying a certain slogan before you or sold a piece of clothing with the slogan on it; what really matters is the one that legally trademarked it. You can trademark things ranging from $100.00 to $1500.00, so why wait when your hundreds of dollars can turn into multi-millions of dollars. Go to the following website for more information TRADEMARK.COM.

23. BRANDING- Branding is your identity and will place you on a map to show others not just who you are, but what you're all about. Branding also identifies you and puts your face on a product. Through your branding, it is very important to know who you are trying to reach and what you are branding. For example, if you are trying to let everyone know that you're a family church or business, don't just put the picture of the pastor or owner on the photo. It is very important that you put a picture of the families if you want to attract singles. Brand singles in your advertisement, if you want to attract a multicultural congregation, then put different nationalities in your advertisement. Too many

times, I have seen pastors and business owners, non-profit and for profit organizations who want to attract a mix of all races of people, but they are only branding one race. People will not hear what you say all the time, but they will respond to what you do. Whatever age you are trying to attract, it is very important that you advertise that age.

If you would like your organization's branding to work effectively, everyone from the pastor to the one sitting in the pew, from the business owner to every staff employee, volunteer or paid, must be on one accord. Other important branding things to remember is one, that your color scheme within your organization's structure, font style in your writing of literature and signage must be consistent. Getting professional pictures taken is also about Branding, because your image is everything. The way you dress, talk, and carry yourself will also determine what kind of people you will attract.

Professional photographers will apply makeup to your face that covers oily skin and blemishes to bring out your natural beauty. Remember, whether you choose an image or not, you have already chosen your image. People will brand you for what you do or not do.

24. PODCAST- Have you ever thought about uploading your effective teachings on the Internet? The Internet connects to millions of people and has enabled almost anyone with a computer to log onto a podcast. Podcasting allows virtually anyone with a computer to hear great teachings. Log on to one of several podcast sites on the Web and you can download content ranging from music, sports and great teachings on a variety of topics. Podcasting is a digital audio technology to create an almost endless supply of content.

Podcasting is a free service that allows Internet users to pull audio files (typically MP3s) from a podcasting website to listen to on their computers or personal digital audio players. The term comes from a combination of the words iPod (a personal digital audio player made by Apple) and broadcasting. Even though the term is derived from the iPod, you don't need an iPod to listen to a podcast. You can use virtually any portable media player or your smart (mobile) phone or computer.

Unlike Internet radio, users don't have to 'tune in' to a particular broadcast. Instead, they download the podcast on demand or subscribe via an RSS (Really Simple Syndication) feed, which automatically downloads the podcast to their computers. Download the podcast app today to your Smartphone and be able to listen to millions of people around the world, or start your own podcast account and upload your own recordings and have people listen to you. This is an excellent way to MARKET YOUR OUTREACH efforts. There are many other applications for podcasting; just turn on your Smartphone and search for podcasting apps or go to PODCAST.com and get started NOW. The world is waiting for YOU!

25. SOCIALCAM- Socialcam is a mobile app that allows you to easily capture and share all of your marketing videos. You can even customize your videos using Socialcam built-in editor with vintage video filters, custom titles, and sound clips.

26. BIG DAYS- Big Days are known as the following: Easter, Mother's Day, Father's Day, Thanksgiving and Christmas. On these five days, make sure you keep everything relevant and relational. BIG days are discussed in the outreach section of THE METHODS OF OUTREACH BOOK.

27. BUS OUTREACH- A bus outreach is one of the most important tools that can be used as a great marketing outreach transportation tool for serving low income individuals and families that are in need of health and human services. I believe that too many people have not experienced growth within their organization, because of a lack bringing people in. If you cannot afford a bus and/or worry about expenses for maintenance, you can always rent a bus and driver and never worry about anything. Call your local charter service or school district TODAY for more information.

28. MASS MAIL- You can mail out a letter to every current resident in your city. One of the first things you have to do is get your non-profit mailing status approved and then go to a title company to request the addresses in the area that you desire to reach. With your 501c3 status, you can mail a letter for less than a third of the price of a regular stamp. Go to or call your local post office TODAY for more information to get started!

29. APARTMENT COMPLEX - apartment complexes are great areas to market, because you get an opportunity to get people who are in transition, such as individuals that have moved from other cities with new jobs or people that are starting over in life. People that live in apartment complexes are often forgot about, but it is the most populated area of people in one spot, even if it is temporary. Most people that live in apartment complexes are there for at least five years, because they're looking to buy a house or improve their lifestyle. To start a successful apartment complex outreach, you first need to contact and build a relationship with the property manager or agency to get permission to place your advertisement into their welcome brochures.

Once a relationship is built, then the office manager can place your brochure inside their welcome package. What are welcome packages? Welcome packages are passed out to potential new residents of the apartment. Included inside the welcome package are the brochures of different restaurants, shopping centers, furniture stores, etc., so placing your church or business advertisement brochure can bring exposure to your organization to people that are in transition. Remember, postcards and flyers must be placed in the manager's office. Most apartment managers do not want churches or businesses passing out flyers to individuals, putting them on cars, or putting door hangers on tenant doors without their consent. Always work within the apartment complex guidelines. You do not have to create your own address, phone or email list. The following company will do this for you for a small fee. InfoUSA is the company that provides you information on apartment complexes in your community. InfoUSA will give you the following data:

1. Name of apartment complex
2. Renters name
3. Address
4. Phone number

If you're interested in finding out more information about InfoUSA, just go to www.infousa.com.

For information on other mail marketing organizations, Google COMPACT INFORMATION SYSTEMS or go to:
www.residentlists.com/SetMainFrame.CF.

30. HOMEOWNERS- you can send a postcard to homeowners in your area not only to give them information about your organization or welcome them into the community or city, but ultimately, to congratu-

late them on the buying of their new home. When a family moves into your area, their primary goal is to get settled in and to do it quickly. They are searching to find new doctors, churches, home service providers and more. You can be the first to welcome them into the community, which could enhance your organization. Even though most people use the four by six postcard size, which is very popular, remember that the six by nine cards are just as good. It's better because it's bigger and takes up more space in the mailbox and can be seen very easily. Postcards allow the new person to get a sneak preview of your organization without even stepping through your doors. One of the first things that most home owners look for when moving into the new community is a church where their children can grow up and where the family can enjoy. This is one of the first steps of the new family getting attached to their community that they now call home. It is very important that you only list answers to questions people are asking or looking for on your postcard, such as the basic services that you offer. Do not put the history of your church or business on the postcard; they will only throw it away. HomeOwner Data Services is a company that provides information all over the country about new homeowners. Once you designate zip codes in your city that you would like to target, HomeOwner Data Services will provide you with the data needed to reach your target audience. Because of HomeOwner Data Services, you now have saved a lot of time and thousands of dollars from doing the work yourself, because the work has already been done for you. Here are some items listed below that HomeOwner Data Services provide to help you grow your organization:

1. Name of the homeowner
2. Spouse's name
3. Date of closing
4. Address
5. Sale price of new home

6. Mortgage amount
7. Estimated income
8. Down payment
9. Subdivision where home is built (If available)
10. Telephone number (If available)
11. Lender name
12. Sales Type (N= brand new home purchase and R=pre-existing home)
13. Seller name

Even though all this information is exciting news, the greatest of all is that it only costs a few cents per house to get this information and it can be shipped right to your office. Once you designate zip codes in your area, HomeOwner Data Services will continue to send you new home-owner information each month until you call and cancel your order. You can check to see if HomeOwner Data Services is offered in your state by going to newhomedata.net.

31. MEMBERSHIP MARKETING- One of the greatest ways to do membership marketing is to have the hospitality department schedule a welcome reception during the week. It is also very important that the lead pastor/general managers, along with associates, are in attendance. If there is a scheduling problem with the pastor/general manager, then the welcome reception should be done when leadership representation is available. This will also allow paid and volunteer staff of your organization to connect with the new members/clientele. Remember, if a person is paid or not, they are still staff.

If they are a volunteer nobody knows but them, so their integrity is to work just like a paid staff. This is how promotion is given. There are four very important things you need to have at your membership marketing event:

1. Food -It is not necessary to have a complete dinner at the event, but finger food appetizers will be acceptable. Remember, you're not there to eat; you're there to build long-lasting relationships with the new members/clientele.

2. Music -A full live band is not necessary. You can keep it as simple as having CD music playing in the background, which will not overwhelm or devalue the moment, but will add value to the moment.

3. Gifts -Everyone loves to receive a gift, so have a drawing to give away special things to local businesses in the community for the new members/customers to use.

4. Photographer -set up a red carpet with a nice background and have a photographer take pictures of the new members/customers, along with the staff, if they would like.

32. MEMBERSHIP RETENTION- once an individual has visited your church/business, they are no longer a visitor; they are now a guest. So your goal now is to connect with them. Following are some key points to keep membership/customer retention:

- It is very important that the pastor/manager personally calls each new member/customer and if it is too time-consuming to make a "Live" call, then use a calling system, such as simple blast, which is a pre-recorded message to call the new member/customer. The phone call should take place within twenty-four hours.

- If there is a dedicated and/or appointed individual to contact the new members/customers within the organization, they should call them as well. Remember, it is imperative that the first voice they hear is from their new pastor/manager.

- Each new member/customer should receive a personalized welcome letter by email and a personal letter by regular mail within forty-eight hours.

- Have someone from the hospitality department drop by their home within seventy-two hours and give the individual or family a gift that they will be able to use. Remember, it is important to be very sensitive to the needs of the household before visiting.

- Once their ministry/department interests that were listed on the new members/customers form has been reviewed, the leader of that ministry/department needs to send them a welcome email within seven days and make sure the welcome email states their meeting schedule and any requirements to be part of that particular ministry/department.

- The assistant administrator/manager of that ministry/department that the new members/customers are involved in should call the new members/customers within fourteen days to make sure they are starting to get connected not only to the church/business, but to some type of involvement within the organization. Remember, this is a process so be very sensitive to the new member/customer. Don't try to rush them.

33. WELCOME VIDEO- Did you know that you can send every member/customer in your church/business a PowerPoint? I believe one of the greatest tools that will work for your organization that will create exposure and not leave out any key details that you would want them to know is a PowerPoint presentation. You can create a three to seven page PowerPoint presentation highlighting key photos and events about your organization. Here is how it's done:

1. Go to SLIDESHARE.NET and establish an account.

2. Email the presentation URL (Address) to each new member.

3. Also post on other social media sites and generate clicks online for your organization.

If Slideshare does not work for you, why don't you try using another website?

1. Go to ANIMOTO.COM and establish an account.

2. Select eight to twenty photos and add them to the presentation.

3. Add your favorite theme or welcome song to the presentation.

4. Upload the video to your YouTube account.

5. Email the link to whoever you would like to receive it.

34. MEAL MARKETING- Hold on and take a timeout; you are raising your stress level trying to call, gather, and schedule everyone to prepare a meal or multiple meals for an individual or family within your church/business. They may be going through tough times in their life, you just want to show an act of kindness or doing it to welcome them into your organization. It does not matter what it is. Now, let me show you how you can work smarter and stop working harder by letting individuals who would like to give a meal, sign up twenty-four hours a day, seven days a week. This means while you're sleeping, the need is still being met simply by turning on their mobile cell device, iPad, notebook or computer and logging onto MAKETHEMAMEAL.COM. Put in the individual or family name that the meal is being prepared for. Once you, as the administrator that built the site, are done, you can text, email, or link your Constant Contact social shares or put it on your Facebook as a link for them to click on, and it will be directed right to the site. There is so much more that this site will do for your organization, but if you do not GO to the site you will never know its potential of helping you to organize the next MEAL MARKETING CAMPAIGN. GET STARTED TODAY! Someone is waiting for you so they can receive a meal TODAY. Also, if you do not have time to cook and deliver a meal, you can pay by credit card and have a meal that is already prepared delivered to the individual or family in need by going to MEALS2GO.COM.

35. APPOINTMENT MARKETING- Are you tired of missing appointments because you can't keep up with the demands and you're not in a good position in this season of your life to have a secretary or administrator for your organization to receive your appointments? Well, stop panicking; I have great news for you. You can have multiple locations and let your clientele members/customers come to you. All you need to do is go to bookfresh.com and let your clients, members, customers schedule their own appointments seven days a week, twenty-four hours a day, depending on your availability and even your location.

36. PARKING LOT- Having parking lot attendees to greet people as they get out of their automobile to come in to your organization is a

very nice first touch for your organization. You can, again, begin with opening up their door for them after their car comes to a stop or provide services, such as parking the car, or umbrellas on a rainy day, just to name few. There are so many ideas that a parking lot attendant can offer, but the most important thing is to have someone visible once your customer arrives. (This topic is expanded more in the outreach book.)

37. GREETERS- The greeters are one of the most important teams in your organization, because they are the first people that not only touch the new and/or repeat customers/members, but they also represent the organization. It does not matter if they are a paid employee or volunteer staff. (This topic is expanded more in the outreach book.)

38. CONNECT CARDS- Connect cards are another great tool for your members/customers to invite people to your organization. All it takes is a business sized card with your time and location on the front and on the back of the card, a place where they will sign their name. (This topic is expanded more in the outreach book.)

39. QR CODES- A QR Code, which is the abbreviation for Quick Response Code, was first designed for the automotive industry in Japan. A barcode is a machine-readable optical label that contains information about the item to which it is attached. A QR Code stores the data to the project in which it is connected to.

The QR Code system became popular outside the automotive industry due to its fast readability and greater storage capacity, compared to standard UPC barcodes. Applications include product tracking, item identification, time tracking, document management, and general marketing. A QR Code can be read by a Smartphone with a camera. The cost is absolutely free to download and create a basic QR generator to your Smartphone and once it is created, you can print it out and placed it on several items, such as your business card, automobile, clothing, banners, stationery, etc. Once the person scans your QR Code, it will take them directly to your organizational website.

Go to QR-CODE-GENERATOR.COM and learn more about how you can receive a quick response from people throughout your city to see what you're actively doing.

40. NEWS WORTHY MARKETING- Contact your local news stations when you are one week away from any of your major outreach events and let them know that your event that is getting ready to happen is a BIG DEAL, because of its impact it has within the community and city. Once the media shows up, you are going to have to be organized and be able to deliver what you said you would do. It is always a great thing when talking to the media to "under promise, but over deliver", but remember that your promise has to be BIG, which will make your delivery even BIGGER. You are going to have to deliver what you said you would, because they will not stay around for something that is not news worthy. Their time is too valuable to be playing games, so unless you are really sure you have a major outreach event, I would wait to call them, because what might be important to you, might not be valuable to them. Just ask yourself this question before you call the media, "What is our organization's competitive advantage? As you continue to keep your consistency, you will grow causing your organization to become BIGGER, BETTER and STRONGER than before.

41. TELEVISION- Commercial, paid programming and/or local free cable access is a great way to put a visual throughout your commu-

nity, city and state to show how your organization is actively impacting, empowering and equipping individuals and families. Before calling the television station, the first thing you need to know before calling is how many commercials that you would like to run on a weekly and/or monthly schedule. For just a few more dollars, you can even boost up the amplifier on the station, so when your commercial comes on, the volume will automatically increase while the viewer is watching. Unless you're a good negotiator, an agent is a great idea to call the station on behalf of your organization to make sure that you receive the best price available on a rotator, which means that your commercial will air throughout the day. All you would have to pay the agency is a percentage of the final cost. Online television is also a great way to market to the social media world and the only cost is the production of the video. Internet television, which is also known as online television, is the digital distribution of television content through the Internet. Internet television is a general term that covers the delivery of television shows and other video content over the Internet by video streaming technology, typically by major traditional television broadcasters, as opposed to traditional systems like terrestrial, cable and satellite, although internet itself is received by terrestrial, cable or satellite methods.

Web television is a term used for programs created by a wide variety of companies and individuals for broadcast on Internet TV. Web TV is original television content produced for broadcast through the World Wide Web. It is a subset, which is part of a larger group of related things of Internet television.

42. ONLINE COURSE- Are you tired of not having enough money to rent out a space to teach others what you have been born to do? Do you have a dream? What are you willing to give up for your dream? Is

your dream bigger than you? Maybe there is something between your dream and your destiny? It can be as simple as a few clicks away to expand what you have been given to expose to others. I believe that you were born to encourage and equip others to do the work they have been given, just as it was given to you. Well, here is the good news I have for you; you can upload your videos and online courses and allow people to step into your virtual classroom from all over the world by enrolling today at UDEMY.COM. I want you to always remember that the promise of your prosperity is always connected to your passion.

43. NEIGHBORHOOD MARKETING- Have you ever said to yourself, "I wish I could meet people throughout my community and city?" It is important to build relationships with those within and around your community, or at least know who they are. Even though there might be a few people throughout your community that would rather be disconnected and isolate themselves, remember, there are hundreds of individuals and families that are waiting to be connected by hearing from you. Have you been waiting a long time for a certain individual to call you? You haven't called them, because the feeling wasn't reciprocated. Finally one day, you said to yourself, "I'm just going to call them, regardless of how I feel and when they finally answered the phone, you could hear the excitement and happiness in their voice. Leaving you in total shock, because you were prepared to say to them, "Why haven't you called me" Your response was, "I wasn't calling you because you weren't calling me." Isn't it amazing how two minds can think the same thing, but never meet? Well, you don't have to wait any longer. Instead of being disconnected from people within your community, you now can be connected to them on purpose. With only a few clicks on your computer, you can meet the person down the street if they have already joined the following website. If not, you can personally invite them to

sign up and always be ready to support each other's events. Are you ready to start building relationships today? Just go to nextdoor.com.

44. EVENT PLANNING- Planning your next event can be as easy as 1, 2, 3. There are many ways that you can plan, such as using some of the websites listed in this chapter, including: CONSTANTCONTACT.COM.

45. BUSINESS CARDS- Your business card is one of the most important parts of your brand identity. It's a common misconception that in the age of Smartphones and social media, the business card is no longer important. Don't believe it! When you meet someone face-to-face, your business card is key to leaving a lasting, positive impression.

Your business card is a relatively small investment that can reap huge rewards – relationships, sales and profits! Through experience, I've learned several ways to maximize the impact a business card can have, and I hope you'll find them helpful.

SEVEN WAYS TO USE YOUR BUSINESS CARD EFFECTIVELY.

1. Invest in quality cards. When you meet someone, your business card continues to represent you long after you depart. A thin card that easily bends, creases, or gets dog ears gives a subtle impression that you're not at the top of your game. Make a strong, lasting impression by using strong card stock and quality printing. It'll cost a little bit more, but it's definitely worth it!

2. Make a card that fits your brand. Your card should be true to your brand identity and appropriate for your field. Style your

card to project the image that you want to portray. If you're an attorney serving corporate clients, then a colorful, glossy card is probably not a good choice. An extreme example, but you get the idea. On the other hand, if you work in a creative field, you can probably be colorful on your cards. Whatever you choose to do, just make sure it represents you, your company and the image you want to convey.

3. Hire a designer. Most printers have business card templates from which you can choose. These work well for a card with a basic layout, but doesn't offer much variety if you want to get a little creative. If you're not a designer yourself, it might not be a good idea to try to create a look yourself. For a layout and design that stands out, using a professional designer can really set your card apart. This doesn't have to cost a lot – you can hire a designer for as low as $5 using online services like FIVERR.COM

4. Drive traffic to your website. Your card should always contain the basics – your name, title, company name, address (if you have one), phone number, email, and website. You don't have to stop with the basics, though – you can use your card to inspire people to visit your website. Give them a compelling reason to pull it up. If you have a free offer on your website, why not feature it on your card? Include a call to action and let them know why they need to be on your website now! In addition to showing your web address on your card, you can add a QR code – that way, all they have to do is scan your card with their Smartphone, and they're taken straight to your website.

5. Create different cards for different audiences. Many entrepreneurs provide different products and services to diverse customer groups. Maybe you have one set of services for consumers, and another for business clients. You can create tailor-made business

cards specifically for your target audience. This way, you can address their specific needs, rather than trying to have a catch-all card. I have several business cards I can choose from, depending upon the situation. I have one card that's all about speaking engagements, one about outreach, one about church and another one about my for profit business.

6. Shop around for a great print shop. If you live in a metropolitan area, there are probably many print shops to choose from. If you don't, it's no problem; you can find a lot of good print shops online. Look for a printer that has testimonials of satisfied customers and examples of their work. Also, make sure their prices are competitive, but be aware that the shop that's the cheapest of the cheap might not provide the level of service you're looking for. I have local printers and online shops I use, depending on the need. I've developed strong relationships with my printers over the years, and it's great to know I can rely on them to turn around a job on a short notice with excellent quality.

7. Always have your cards on-hand. There's nothing worse than making an important connection and not having your business card with you. Safeguard against this by keeping your cards handy at all times. Invest in several business-card holders so they stay pristine. Keep cards in your purse, briefcase, your car's glove compartment, at your office and at home. Make it a habit to grab your cards when you get your phone – if you're like me, this will keep them with you at all times!

Take a look at your business card. Does it convey who you are, and what your brand is all about? Is it high quality? Is it professionally designed and visually appealing? Does it give a compelling reason to get connected with you and visit your website? If not, consider upgrading your cards. It could increase the quality of your connections and your profits!

Think of all the places you can hand out or leave your business card. Make it a point to get your card in the hands of potential customers, clients or business partners every day this week. Start giving out your business cards today as if big things are on the way, because they are! Go somewhere you've never been and meet some new people. You have to change your comfort zone to change your money zone! You'll start seeing results quickly.

46. GOOGLE PLUS- Google+ is a place to connect with friends and family, and explore all of your interests. Set up a Google+ account and invite all your friends, family and new members and clients to your network. You can engage in conversations with everyone in your circle once a day, once a week or as much as you want. Send out email announcements through the circle also and once you set up the circle, you don't have to input their email address. It's as easy as 1, 2, 3 to send an update to the entire circle by hitting "send" one time. Just go to GOOGLE.COM and sign up today!

47. VIRTUAL BUSINESS- If you're on the go all the time or stationary, you can have a professional virtual office local or toll-free number and much more for a small monthly fee. Get started today by going to GRASHOPPER.COM or ONECALLNOW.COM and let them do all the work for you. It doesn't matter if you're a pastor of a church, a coach of a local sports team, a medical doctor or a business owner; this system will work for everyone! Remember, it will work if you work it and it's not about you working harder, but working smarter.

48. ONLINE MEETINGS- Do you want your meetings to be conducted with everyone involved without the stress of calling everyone individually? Get ready, get set and...GOTOMEETING.COM!

49. PAYROLL- You don't have to keep trying to do staff payroll all by yourself and worrying about if you are keeping up with IRS regulations. Don't put your organization in jeopardy. There are businesses that can keep you legal. Logon to PAYCHEX.COM or ADP.COM.

50. SKYPE- Would you like to stay in contact with family, friends and business connections across the world for free? Through videos, you can show and tell about all the excitement that is happening within your organization. Go to SKYPE.COM and start connecting today!

51. LINKEDIN- You can get and stay connected to all your networking business professionals and give and receive personalized insights about you and the people you want to stay connected with. You no longer have to be the missing link. Go to LINKEDIN.COM and start your professional profile TODAY!

52. FLICKR- (pronounced "flicker") is an image hosting and video hosting website, and web services suite. Flickr is probably one of the best online photo management and sharing application in the world today. It also allows you to make your photos and videos available to everyone, as well as organize them. Part of the solution is to make the process of organizing photos or videos collaborative. In Flickr, you can give your friends, family, and other contacts permission to organize your stuff- not just to add comments, but also notes and tags. Go to FLICKR.com today so you can start to market the photos and videos of all your outreach events. Another creative idea to experience long-lasting memories is by creating a photo album of all your outreach events; you can even create cards and stationary, as well as share all your prints for a reasonable price at SHUTTERFLY.COM.

CHAPTER FOUR

DIGITAL AND NON-DIGITAL MARKETING

1. What are digital footprints?

    _____

    _____

2. What are the two main classifications for digital footprints?

    - _____
    - _____

3. How are passive digital footprints created?

    _____

    _____

4. How are active digital footprints created?

    _____

    _____

5. What are non-digital footprints?

    _____

    _____

6. Non-digital marketing is also known as:

    _____

7. List ten digital footprints:

    • _____

    • _____

    • _____

    • _____

    • _____

    • _____

    • _____

    • _____

    • _____

- _____

8. List ten non-digital footprints:

- _____

- _____

- _____

- _____

- _____

- _____

- _____

- _____

- _____

- _____

Chapter 5
Power of Partnership

TWO OF THE GREATEST enhancements to knowing how to market your outreach are first, understanding the meaning of the words partnership and networking. Partnership can either take away or add value to your outreach marketing plans. This is why being in unity and harmony with the individual or organization you are partnering with can make a big difference in not only how affective you are, but also your effectiveness. You can always hide the affect of being out of tune, but you cannot hide the effectiveness of the rhythm of the organization. Plottage might be a certain value of a property, but when you connect the property to the property on the left and the right, it is now called assemblage, which means its original value has now increased, because of its growth in size.

As an organization, you have a specific calling and once you hook up and connect with like-minded people that are going in the same direction you are going, you will always win- every time. I highly recommend that you don't spend a lot of time always focusing on your losses, but stay forward focused on the destination, so you can arrive at the finish line. The right partnership in your life will always add value to whatever you're doing and in return, not only one person will win, but everyone wins. The real question you might be wondering right now is what is partnership? A partnership is an arrangement where parties agree to cooperate to advance their mutual interests.

Since we are social beings, partnerships between individual, business, interest-based organizations, schools, governments and a variety of combinations will always remain a commonplace. A partnership is formed between one or more businesses in which partners' co-labor to achieve and share profit and losses. Partnership exists within and across non-profit and for profit organizations that are partnered together to increase the likelihood of their outreach marketing to achieve their mission.

Partnerships always start at a personal level, such as when two or more individuals agree to share domicile together. It is very dangerous for you to even consider connecting with another individual or organization that cannot enhance what you have been designed to do. The bottom line is if it does not add value to your organization, it is subtracting from it. Be very careful of individuals of organizations that are sponges in your life, which means they are soaking everything up from you, but not giving anything back in return.

CHAPTER FIVE

POWER OF PARTNERSHIP

1. Partnerships can either _____ away or _____ value to your outreach marketing.

2. What is the definition of the word partnership?

    _____

    _____

3. How are partnerships formed?

    _____

    _____

4. What is the purpose of two organizations, non-profit and for profit, partnering together?

    _____

    _____

5. Make a list of ten organizations you would like to partner with:

    *   _____

    *   _____

- _____

- _____

- _____

- _____

- _____

- _____

- _____

- _____

Chapter 6
Networking

JUST LIKE PARTNERSHIP is powerful; networking is just as powerful for your organization. The right partnership can add value to your organization, but networking will always enhance the value that has been added. Several years ago, a powerful statement was downloaded into my spirit, as I began to network with other organizations: If you are not networking, you are not working". For years, I have held onto this quote. What is a NET? A net can be considered an interlocking or intertwining of individuals who are related to one another through mutual contacts. This means one person is connected to another who is directly connected to someone else, and it keeps on going. What is

WORK? Work is a common word, but once it is connected to the word NET, it now becomes an action word, such as "NETWORK". A network is a group or system of interconnected people or things, or a group of people who exchange information, contacts and experiences for professional or social purpose.

To have your network work effectively for your organization, you have to put in the work to get the results you want or it will never work. If you don't work it, it will never work." A lot of outreach organizations expect to receive something without putting in the work, but you have to stay connected to the source, which causes your resources to flow. Now that we have looked at the word "NET" and the word "WORK", now let's take a close look at the last part of the abbreviation of the word networking, which is "ING". The acronym is "I"nviting "N"ew "G"uests. It is verbal action or results. Now that you have extended your net, you can expect your organization to grow. Now let's take a look at what the word networking means. Networking is interacting with other people to exchange information and developing contacts, especially to further one's career. It is also used to make contact in business for the purpose beyond the reason of initial contact. The real question is what does networking mean to you? Over the years, I've heard many people make statements such as, "I know so many people, but it never gets me anywhere." The problem with this statement could be that it's not who you know, but what and who they know that can make a tremendous difference in the value of the networking relationship. Maybe you're just hanging around too many people that have your problem and not your answer. It's not always about the quantity of people that you know; it's also about the quality of the people you know. The following are three key questions that you might want to ask yourself when networking:

- Am I more interested in the other person, or am I just talking about myself?
- Am I talking negative gossip, or does my conversing in conversation add value to the other person?
- Am I a liability or asset to this person?

Take a good look at your answers, as they may reveal the problem in your outreach marketing efforts. If you continue to do the same thing, the same negative way, you're always going to get the same negative results. But if you change your thinking process, positive things will happen. The mindset of a successful network is to provide value to others and not just always getting business or help for themselves. In order for you to have a great outreach marketing organization, you have to gain the respect and trust of others, which will often translate into success and credibility.

ELEVEN KEY OUTREACH MARKETING POINTS A NETWORKER NEEDS

1. Are you authentic and true to your word?
2. Are you consistent in both what you say and do?
3. Do you lose focus in times of trouble, hardship or temptation?
4. Are you passionate and do you speak from the heart, while allowing your listener to speak and be heard as well?
5. Are you outgoing?
6. Are you sincere?
7. Are you friendly?
8. Are you supportive?
9. Are you a good listener?
10. Do you follow up and stay in touch with people?

11. Do you give other people referrals and ideas without thinking about your own personal gain?

If you would just apply these eleven simple key points to your outreach marketing, you will experience success in everything you do. The ability to network is one of the most important tools in any outreach marketing plan, because it will provide you the contacts that are necessary to grow your organization. Many people go to networking events, but very few know how to network effectively. Networking is more than just getting out and meeting people; it is a structured plan to get to know people who will do business with you or introduce you to other people who will do business with you. The best way to have continued success in your outreach efforts is to make a plan. If you fail to plan, then you are planning to fail. Commit to your plan no matter who says it's not going to work. Remember, if you live by their compliments, you will give up because of their criticism. Last but not least, you have to execute the plan in good or bad times.

Now that you have a plan, as I previously stated, you have to stay committed and cultivate it until it grows. Fifty percent of successful networking is reaching out. This is why it is called OUTreach marketing, because you have to go out to see your results and not stay within the four walls of your organization. Just because you attend several networking groups does not mean your organization will become successful. If you continue always meeting with the same people, you will continue to get the same results. You have to be willing to expand your territory, in order to receive continued growth. Also, another key to successful networking is to always be proactive. Being reactive causes you to become confused on what to do once you attend a networking event. When you're proactive, you have to cause something to happen, instead of being reactive after it has already happened. Being proactive will prevent any potential problems. When you are reactive, you are responding to a problem within your organization and trying to control it. It could've been avoided if you would have just taken the time out to be proactive, saving yourself a lot of heartache and stress.

SEVEN KEYS TO NETWORKING

Remember, if you're not "NETWORKING", you're NOT working!

1. Set a goal to meet a certain amount of people at every networking event that you attend.

2. Always look for people you have never met and let it become a habit. If you don't, you will always naturally gravitate toward people that you already know.

3. Attend multiple networking groups. This way you will not only expand your networking efforts, but you will also be able to find your niche. Always be willing to expose your organization, because "What you don't expose will never expand."

4. Carry your business cards with you all the time. You never know when you might be connected with a current contact, but if you don't have your cards with you, it is a guarantee you will be disconnected from a future contact.

5. Stay active. When attending a networking event, don't just go sit down in a chair. You have to get involved in the inner workings of the group, because it will always cause you to have great visibility throughout the group. Remember, people are always looking for someone to be an "asset, not a liability."

6. Be friendly and approachable. Always act like you're the host of any networking event you attend. This will always cause people to feel welcomed whenever they meet you, and in return, they

will always introduce you to other contacts, as well. If you would consistently stay focused on helping others, soon you will find other people helping you.

7. Be willing to be a giver, so you can be a receiver. Networking is a bilateral relationship; don't expect new contacts if you're not willing to give any out.

Other terminology for Network Marketing is social and attraction. Social Marketing and Attraction Marketing are both network marking tools. Social outreach marketing is the ability to reach out to potential and existing customers using social media technology. It helps everyone to interact with each other. Attraction outreach marketing is the ability for people to reach in, as potential customers, and search out your organization. Remember, "facts tell and stories sell." Your facts will always provide the proof and your stories will always tell the truth.

Some of the most successful people in networking are the ones that not only talk about the events, but actually show up at the networking events. The first three letters in the word actually spells "ACT", which means you have to do something to get results. People that show up to these events are people that are committed to finding answers and are willing to do what it takes to solve their and/or the organizationan's problems. As a leader, it is very important for you to get out of your comfort zone and go to conferences that will empower and equip you to be the best you. It's totally up to you; no one's going to make you do it. They only can suggest that you do it, but you are the one that has to make the move. When you become distracted trying to answer questions that no one is asking, you are hindering your own personal knowledge, which will affect organizational success. When you stop pursuing, it slows down your progress, which will eventually limit your potential. It's very important for you to know when the light is RED, YELLOW or GREEN.

SIX KEYS TO "NOT WORKING"

Remember, if you're not "networking", you're "NOT WORKING"

1. Afraid to go by yourself.

   Most people that are starting non-profit or for profit organizations use this excuse all the time. If this is true, then they are a great candidate to go to the networking event, because as we can see, they definitely need a friend!

2. Afraid to meet new people.

   I do understand that some people are very shy and uncomfortable at social events, but I want you to realize that you were made to be an Overcomer and a conqueror. It is the confronting that is standing in your way of elevating knowledge and organizational success. You will never be able to conquer things that you cannot confront. Have you ever stopped just for a moment to realize what would happen if you showed up to a networking event full of successful business people that you have never met and you sit next to someone and started to engage in a conversation and they offer the answer to your problem? You never know what people can do for you and what you can do for them, unless you make a move. What great connections are you missing out on by skipping networking events? No successful student ever passes their class by skipping the class. It is vitally important that you attend the class no matter how you feel, especially if you want to graduate to the next level.

3. Online connections are not all you need.

Social media is an amazing and powerful tool for personal and business connections, but social connections can never replace personal connections. What social media does offer is a connection with people that you would probably never meet throughout your daily routine. Once you meet a person on social media, as a source, the power of connecting comes when you meet face to face, which can perhaps cause a short-term or lifelong partnership. You will never receive power for what you're called to do, until you get plugged into the power source of networking. So, get out of your seat, on your feet and in the streets and start making connections today!

4. You don't know it all.

Most people think they know everything about their business. Just because you have read some books, been to a few conferences and gotten some years of experience, don't ever think that there's nothing else for you to learn, because once you stop learning, you will stop earning.

5. STOP and get some HELP!

Have you ever felt like you have a lot to learn about how to network for your organization? Well, I have some great news for you! Stop feeling ashamed and embarrassed and open up your mouth and ask for help. Most people don't ask for help, because they feel like they should be further along in their organization, or they believe it's a sign of showing weakness. If this is your attitude, I would like to drop some knowledge on you. All successful people get consistent help. Most leaders CEOs, executives, pastors, managers, directors and so on, have monthly mentors and committed coaching. It is vitally important that you get around people that have your answer and not your problem.

6. Stop worrying about who gets the credit.

Showing up to someone else's event does not mean that it validates their success; it might be just what you need to begin, enhance or validate your own success. The truth is they are going to be successful whether you show up to the event or not. Don't let your insecurities hold you back from achieving your highest level of success.

So what are you going to do, own up to what you're called to do or are you going to keep making excuses as to why you can't do what you're called to do? My advice to you is to not have a stay in the boat mentality, become focused on what's ahead. Don't let distractions detour you from your destiny; start walking on some water and show up to every networking event and conference possible that pertains to where you're going.

CHAPTER SIX

NETWORKING

1. Networking will always _____the _____that has been added.

2. Finish the following quote: "If you're not _____, you're not _____."

3. What is the definition of a net?

   _____

   _____

4. What is the definition of work?

    _____

    _____

5. Is the word network an action word? (Yes/No)_____

6. What is the definition of the word network?

    _____

    _____

    _____

7. What does the acronym "ING" means when connected to the word "networking"?

    I _____

    N _____

    G _____

8. What is the definition of the word networking?

    _____

    _____

    _____

9. What is your definition of networking in regards to your organizational structure?

_____

_____

_____

_____

10. It is not always about the _____ of people that you know; it's about the _____ of people you know.

11. What are the following three questions you need to ask yourself before engaging in a network conversation?

- _____

- _____

- _____

12. The mindset of a successful networker is to provide _____ to others and not just always getting business for yourself.

13. The trust of other people will always translate into the _____ and _____ of yourself.

14. What are the eleven keys to outreach marketing?

- _____

- _____

- _____

- _____

- _____

- _____

- _____

- _____

- _____

- _____

- _____

15. Fifty percent of successful networking is reaching out; that's why it is called _____marketing.

16. In networking, you have to be proactive, so you do not become _____.

17. What is the definition of being proactive?

_____

18. What is the definition of being reactive?

_____

19. What is the reward for being proactive?

_____

20. What are the seven keys to Networking?

• _____

• _____

• _____

• _____

• _____

• _____

• _____

21. What are the six keys to "Not Working"?

- _____

- _____

- _____

- _____

- _____

- _____

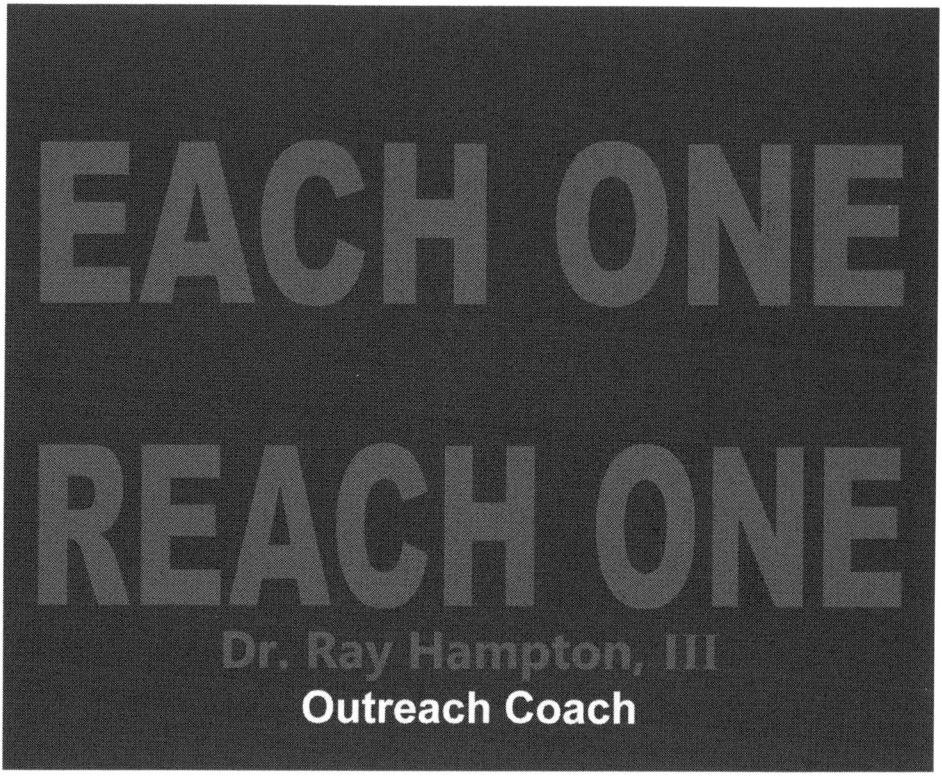
EACH ONE
REACH ONE
Dr. Ray Hampton, III
Outreach Coach

What Is "Each One Reach One"?

The word *Each* means everyone individually or one by one. To *Reach* is to stretch or extend as to touch or meet. Another definition would be to succeed in making contact with influencing, impressing, interesting or convincing. When looking at the word *One* it means to be considered as a single unit or individually.

Mission/Vision

Equip Members
To Make Disciples

Philosophy Pyramid

EACH ONE

REACH ONE

WON *by* ONE

Success is only measured by a transformed life

PRODUCE

You Can Do It

PRODUCTIVITY

Confidence & Trust

- Stay motivated
- Don't give up
- Do the right thing because it's the right thing to do
- Work smarter not harder
- Be an asset and not a liability
- Aim don't shoot

Effectiveness

PERSISTENCE

- Affectiveness stirs things up but Effectiveness gets results
- How can you lead where you do not go or teach what you do not know
- You have to compete to complete
- The result of labor is favor
- Goals without dates are dreams
- Practice is not just perfect, it's permanent

Belief System

PASSION

- Do what you have to do so you can do what you need to do
- Proper planning prevents poor performance
- If you are not networking you are NOT working
- Get around people that have your answer and not your problem
- Focus on the one and not the thousand

THE REACH CYCLE

OUTREACH

Plant   Serve   Sowing

INREACH

Water   Teach   Cultivate

RE-REACH

Grow   Release   Reaping

PHILOSOPHY

The general principles or a particular system of a field of knowledge for the conduct of life.

PRODUCE

To produce, as a verb, is to give birth to a produce (noun). It also means to have a cause and effect of a product. The product is the result of your productivity and will cause birth to a production of something else.

PRODUCTIVITY

Productivity is to fertilize and to be fruitful. It is the act of producing or the giving and putting out your effort to see an increasing product come to realization.

PERSISTENCE

To be persistent is refusing to give up and have patience toward a certain goal even when you are faced with opposition and going through adversity. It's having the endurance and the ability to bear the pain without flinching.

PASSION

To be passionate is to have an intense emotional excitement. It is to be enthusiastic, have a continued zeal, strong desire and feeling toward something. When you are passionate about something you will have a craving and stirring up within yourself.

6 Principles of Learner

SILENT

To not make a vocal sound. To be quiet and to be still.
The reason you have two ears and one mouth is so you can listen more than you talk.

LISTEN

To pay attention and wait attentively for a sound so that you will remember what you have heard. If your mouth is speaking your ears are not hearing. Be slow to speak and quick to listen.

REMEMBER

To refresh and update your memory of what you have heard before.

UNDERSTAND

The power to think . learn and comprehend.
What you don't know CAN hurt you.

JUDGEMENT

The ability to make a sound decision.

ACTION

Is not just be a hearer but a doer.

FOUR TYPES OF PEOPLE IN THE WORLD

1. People who **make** things happen
2. People who **watch** things happen
3. People who **let** things happen
4. People who **ask** what happen

THE 'TATOR' FAMILY

- **Commentators**
  People that show up at community events, rallies and meetings but never do anything but talk.
- **Spectators**
  Always see things in the community but never do anything in the community. Yet, like commentators, they always have something to say.
- **Non-Participators**
  These people are physically at community meetings but are mentally thinking about something else.
- **Irritators**
  These are people that are all of the above and just simply get on everybody's nerve.
- **Participators**
  Are people who get the job done.

VOCALIZE

To **vocalize** something is to SAY IT!

VISUALIZE

To **visualize** something in your life is to
SEE IT!

MEMORIZE

To **memorize** something is to THINK IT!

MOBILIZE

To **mobilize** something is to DO IT!

Product Page

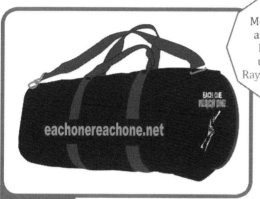

$ 55.00

More Products
are available.
Please visit
us online at
RayHampton.com

$ 15.00

Also
available
in black

Made in the USA
Columbia, SC
20 December 2017